Tracing Your Irish Roots

First published in 2009 by
Appletree Press Ltd
The Old Potato Station
14 Howard St South
Belfast BT7 1AP

Tel.: +44 (0) 28 9024 3074
Fax: +44 (0) 28 9024 6756
Email: reception@appletree.ie
Web: www.appletree.ie

A catalogue record for this book is available from the British Library.

First published as *Tracing Your Irish Roots* in 1999 by Appletree Press

Tracing Your Irish Roots

ISBN: 978 1 84758 122 8

Desk and Marketing Editor: Jean Brown
Copy-editor: Jim Black
Designer: Stuart Wilkinson
Production Manager: Paul McAvoy

9 8 7 6 5 4 3 2 1

AP3605

Tracing Your Irish Roots

Christine Kinealy

Contents

Introduction

Have you ever wondered about your forebears – where they lived, what their occupations were, how many children they had? Are you perhaps a descendant of Brian Boru, or of a 17th-century Scottish 'planter'? Perhaps your great-grandfather was hanged for stealing sheep, or maybe your grandmother was a Poor Law Guardian? Knowledge of your family history will not only answer these and many other questions but it will also give you a greater understanding of Irish history and show the part that your ancestors have played in it.

Over the last few years there has been a great increase in the number of people who want to find out more about their roots. Unfortunately, the pathway to the past can sometimes be rocky. Where do you start? What records and documents do you need? What information do they contain and where are they kept? And what do you do if you come to an apparent dead end?

This book will show you how to undertake a genealogical search and develop it as far as possible. Parish registers, census returns, gravestone inscriptions, newspapers and birth, death and marriage certificates – all these can contain vital information about your ancestors. And each can provide you with that crucial link to the next stage of your search. Success or failure can hinge on something seemingly unimportant. For example, suppose you are looking for ancestors with the surname Sullivan. If you have done your homework, you will know that this surname originally had the prefix 'O' – a simple yet vital piece of information.

Surname, religion, place of origin and occupation will provide clues that are all too easily overlooked by the untrained eye. Essentially, family history is a question of knowing which plot of earth is the most appropriate in which to sink your genealogical spade to commence root digging!

Starting Off

Any genealogical search should begin at home. In fact, by devoting time to this important stage, you will probably save valuable time later in your search. On a large piece of paper, near the bottom, write your name. Then construct a line chart of your parents, grandparents and so on. You should end up with something like this:

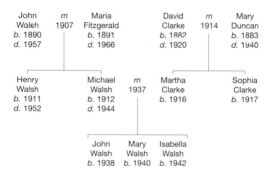

| John Walsh b. 1890 d. 1957 | m 1907 | Maria Fitzgerald b. 1891 d. 1966 | | David Clarke b. 1882 d. 1920 | m 1914 | Mary Duncan b. 1883 d. 1940 |

| Henry Walsh b. 1911 d. 1952 | Michael Walsh b. 1912 d. 1944 | m 1937 | Martha Clarke b. 1916 | Sophia Clarke b. 1917 |

| John Walsh b. 1938 | Mary Walsh b. 1940 | Isabella Walsh b. 1942 |

This simple family tree will help to show you the gaps in your knowledge. You may not be able to go much beyond your grandparents' generation. And it is quite probable that you don't even know your grandmother's maiden name. You may also be uncertain about exact dates of birth, death and marriage. However, don't despair! Once you have realised the extent and limits of your knowledge, you will have a much clearer idea of the task ahead.

The next step is to try to fill in the gaps. Collect together as much family memorabilia as you can. Diaries, family bibles, newspaper cuttings, photographs – they all have a story to tell. Keep them together. Even if they don't contribute anything immediately, they may be useful at a later stage.

Finally, approach other members of your family, particularly older relatives, and close family friends and see what they can remember. Before long, you should have collected a wealth of interesting information. However, don't take every thing at face value: memories are notoriously unreliable so, wherever possible, check dates and ages against other sources. A golden rule of family history is to write everything down. Do this from the very start of your search. If you don't, you will regret it later.

Surnames

Everybody has a surname. When trying to trace your family history, identification by surname is the first stage in locating and identifying your ancestors because a surname provides that vital link with the past. So, at an early stage in your search, it is worth spending time finding out as much as possible about the origin and history of your surname. If, for example, you discover that your surname is of Gaelic, Norman, Huguenot, Scottish or Jewish origin, it will provide you with information that could prove invaluable in guiding you to the relevant records. So knowing as much as possible about your surname is an important part of any genealogical search.

The surnames found in Ireland today reflect its rich history and the variety of people who have settled in the country. Ireland was, in fact, one of the first countries to develop a system of hereditary surnames – names, that is, that were handed down from one generation to another. They began to be widely used in the 11th century as the population grew and first names became an insufficient means of identification.

At first, Irish surnames were formed by adding, for example, 'Mac' to the father's personal name or 'O' to that of any earlier ancestor. For example, 'O'Neil' simply meant 'descendant of Niall (Neil)'. After a while, however, other types of surnames were adopted which were not based on personal names, for example 'Mac Nulty', which meant 'son of the Ulsterman'.

The surnames found in Ireland today have many diverse origins. The first group of settlers who had an impact on surnames was the Anglo-Normans. They came to Ireland in the 12th century. Although the Anglo-Normans integrated quickly into Irish society, they brought with them their own distinctive surnames. These surnames included Fitzgerald, Butler, Power and Walsh – names now numerous in all parts of Ireland.

The next important settlement occurred in the 16th century when large areas of land, mainly in the Midlands of

Ireland, were confiscated by the English government and English families were 'planted' (or settled) on them. Names such as Spenser, Hyde and Browne became established in Ireland at this time.

At the beginning of the 17th century, a much larger settlement took place when people from Scotland and England were encouraged by the government in London to purchase land in some parts of Ulster. Thousands of people took advantage of this and migrated to Ulster. These people were known as 'planters'. Many of them were Presbyterian. As a result of this 'plantation', names such as Graham, Patterson, Ferguson, Kerr and Stewart became numerous in the north eastern part of Ulster, particularly in counties Antrim and Down.

As English and Scottish influence spread in the 17th century, many old Irish surnames were anglicised. This was done in a variety of ways. Some surnames were translated into the new English equivalent or were changed to a similar sounding English name. The prefixes 'O' and 'Mac' were frequently dropped in an attempt to make them sound more English. Thus Mac anGhabhonn (son of the Smith) was variously rendered as MacGowan, Gowan or Smith. This process of Anglicisation occurred in a haphazard way over a number of years and gave rise to many variants in the spelling of a surname. As a consequence, a surname might assume different forms in different areas. This has also served to obscure the real origin of the surnames.

Towards the end of the 17th century, another group of immigrants settled in Ireland. These were the Huguenots – French Protestants escaping from religious persecution in their own country. Their main areas of settlement were Dublin, Portarlington and Lisburn. Their legacy survives in the surnames Fontaine, D'Ollier, La Touche and Refausse.

Two other important settler groups contributed to the variety of 'Irish' surnames. The first of these was the Palatine Germans, who came to Ireland at the beginning of the 18th century and contributed names such as Switzer, Ruttle and

Boveniser. The second was a large group of Jews from Eastern Europe, who also came to Ireland to escape religious persecution, at the end of the 19th century. Their surnames are distinctive and include Jaffe, Cohen, Greenburg and Heiner.

The process of Anglicisation, combined with the fact that before the 20th century illiteracy was widespread, means that many Irish surnames can be spelt in a variety of ways. Consider, for example, the surname Johnston. Variants of this include Johnstone, Johnston, Johnson, MacEion (son of John), MacOwen, MacKeon, and MacKeown. The surname Kearns can be variously rendered as Cairns, Carns, Cearnes, Kerns and Kearnes.

Many Irish surnames are associated with particular areas. For example, the surname McNell is found in County Donegal, while O'Sullivan is traditionally associated with West Cork. In the case of unusual surnames, this can sometimes provide you with a starting point for your search. But you must not assume that all people with the same surname within an area are necessarily your ancestors. They may be, but any suspected links should, as far as possible, be substantiated by other forms of evidence.

Before starting your family history it is vital to familiarise yourself with all the variants of the surnames in which you are interested. Make a list of the variants and refer to it when searching any indexes or records. Before the 20th century, however, there was little standardisation in the spelling of a surname. A person baptised George Burn could be married as George Bearn and buried as George Burns. Bear in mind also that a person who was known all her life as Sophia Kelly may appear in official records as Mary Sophia Kelly.

Places and Place Names

When trying to trace your ancestors in Ireland, it is important to have as precise an idea as possible about their place of origin. Occasionally, if you only know their county of origin, this may be sufficient to locate them but, in general, the more precise you can be about their address, the better.

Townlands, streets or parish addresses are the most common – and most useful – means of identification. Surnames too, particularly unusual ones, can sometimes provide a clue to a family's place of origin. If you know, for example, that your grandfather, Desmond Quiery, lived in the townland of Drumbrughas in 1890, it is useful to find out as much about that area as possible. To do this, consult *The Alphabetical Index to the Townlands and Towns of Ireland*, available in any good reference library. From it you will see that Drumbrughas is a townland in Carly, Fermanagh, in the barony of Clanawley, the parish of Killesher, the county district of Enniskillen and the district electoral division of Drumane. Its size is 216 acres, 15 perches and its reference number for Ordnance Survey Maps is 33. Write this down, as this information will prove very helpful later in your search.

The address is a basic unit of identity but it can take a variety of forms. It is therefore invaluable to familiarise yourself with the different locations used. Different records are categorised by various geographic divisions and these names will provide the necessary key to using the correct records. The following are the main geographic and administrative units in Ireland:

Provinces: there were originally five of these but there are only four in modern Ireland – Ulster in the north; Leinster in the east; Munster in the south, and Connaught in the west. The province is the largest geographic division in Ireland.

Counties: the system of 'shiring' Ireland started in the 12th century as English influence spread throughout Ireland.

Ulster was the last part of the country to be shired and was divided into counties Coleraine, Tyrone, Fermanagh, Cavan, Monaghan, Armagh, Antrim, Down and Donegal. County Coleraine was subsequently renamed County Londonderry. Only six of these Ulster counties form Northern Ireland – the remaining three (Cavan, Donegal and Monaghan) are in the Republic of Ireland.

Baronies: baronies are subdivisions of counties. As an administrative unit they have been obsolete for about a century, but between 1600-1900 they were frequently used as a unit by the government for carrying out surveys.

Parishes: since the religious Reformation of the 16th century, there have been two separate parish structures in Ireland; civil and Roman Catholic. The term 'civil parish' refers to the parish of the Established Church in Ireland – that is, the Church of Ireland. This Church remained the state Church until 1869.

Townlands: you will frequently come across this term in your research. A townland is the smallest administrative unit in Ireland. It does not relate to a town. There are about 64,000 townlands in Ireland. Traditionally, in rural areas, people identified closely with their townland and it is therefore the basic form of address provided in many records. Townlands are not static: over the years, there have been divisions (usually into Upper and Lower) and amalgamations and changes in townland names (e.g. Lisnagarvey is now known as Lisburn), and, like names, the spelling can differ (e.g. Tandragee/Tanderagee). A valuable record of townlands exists in the Ordnance Survey Townland Maps (scale: 6 inches to 1 mile).

County Districts Areas: these have a separate council and date from the late 19th century.

District Electoral Divisions: these consist of a group of townlands clustered together.

Ward Administrative Division: these exist within a city or large town. An address, therefore, is a unit of identity, which will help you to identify your ancestor and obtain further information about him or her. However, the address given on a document can take a variety of forms, and if you are aware of this, it will make your search more rewarding as it will allow you to use a wide variety of records to their best advantage.

Useful Depositories

From the time of the Viking invasion of Ireland in the 8th century until the 20th century, the administrative centre for the thirty-two counties of Ireland was Dublin. The Act of Union of 1800 (by which Ireland lost its own parliament in Dublin) shifted some administrative responsibility to London. Also as a consequence, the United Kingdom of Great Britain and Ireland was created. The partition of Ireland in 1921 changed the situation again. Six counties in the north east of Ireland (Antrim, Armagh, Londonderry, Down, Fermanagh and Tyrone) remained as part of the United Kingdom and the other twenty-six counties were constituted into the Irish Free State. As a result, the administrative centre for Northern Ireland became Belfast (and, at times, London) while Dublin continued as the administrative centre for the other twenty-six counties. After 1949, the Free State became known as the Republic of Ireland.

For genealogists and family historians, the effects of the partition of Ireland can be confusing. After 1921, a Public Record Office (PRONI) and a Registrar-General's Office (GRO) was established in Belfast, so records for an Irish ancestor might be located in Dublin or Belfast depending on place of origin, date of birth or death, and so on.

Record Depositories in the Republic of Ireland

The National Archives of Ireland (NAI)

Until 1988 this office was known as the Public Record Office of Ireland and it was situated at the Four Courts, Dublin. In 1988, the Public Record Office and the State Paper Office were amalgamated to form the National Archives of Ireland.

The original Public Record Office was destroyed by fire in 1922 during the Irish Civil War. However, despite the loss of many records, it continued to provide an excellent resource for the family historian. The most frequently consulted records were moved to the new offices in Bishop St. Records from the State Paper Office in Dublin Castle were also moved to this location. Material of genealogical value to be found at the National Archives includes:

> 1901 and 1911 census returns
> Griffith's *Valuation*
> Tithe Applotment Books
> some Church of Ireland parish registers
> school registers
> trade union archives
> abstracts of indexes of wills.

The Tithe Applotment Books and Griffith's *Valuation* can only be consulted on microfilm.

The full address of the National Archives is:
> The National Archives, 8 Bishop St, Dublin 8
> Telephone: +353 (0) 1 407 2300
> Fax: +353 (0) 1 407 2333
> Email: mail@nationalarchives.ie
> Website: www.nationalarchives.ie

State Paper Office
Since 1988, the State Paper Office has been part of the National Archives. It contains records relating to the administration of Ireland from approximately 1790 to 1922. This includes:

> police and crime records
> convict reference files
> rebellion papers
> documents relating to transportation and
>   State-sponsored emigration.

The full address is the same as for the National Archives.

The National Library
The National Library incorporates the office of the Chief Herald and the State Heraldic Museum and contains records relating to pedigrees, coats of arms and heraldic certificates. The library has microfilm copies of all Roman Catholic parish registers up to 1880. It also has an excellent newspaper collection and copies of Griffith's *Valuation* and the Ordnance Survey Books. The library has an extensive collection of pamphlets, street directories and genealogical reference books. It also offers a free genealogical advice service for visitors.

The full address is:
  The National Library, Kildare St, Dublin 2
  Telephone: +353 (0) 1 603 0200
  Fax: +353 (0) 1 661 2523
  Email: info@nli.ie
  Website: www.nli.ie

The Office of the Registrar-General
This office contains records of:
  births, deaths and marriages for all of Ireland
    from 1864 to 1921
  records of non-Catholic marriages after 1845
  births, deaths, and marriages for the Republic of
    Ireland from 1864 to the present day.

All enquiries should be addressed to:
  General Register Office, Government Offices
  Convent Road, Roscommon
  Telephone: +353 (0) 90 663 2900
  Fax: +353 (0) 90 663 2999 / +353 (0) 90 663 2988
  Website: www.groireland.ie

A self-service search facility is available at:
  The Office of the Registrar-General
  3rd Floor, Block 7
  Irish Life Centre, Lower Abbey St, Dublin 1
  Contact via www.groireland.ie for details.

The Property Registration Authority

There are two separate systems for recording transactions in relation to property in Ireland:

1. The Registration of Title system operated by the Land Registry since 1892
2. The Registry of Deeds system operated by the Registry of Deeds since 1708

Both systems are under the control of the *Property Registration Authority* which was established in November 2006 under the provisions of the Registration of Deeds and Title Act 2006. The records of the Registry of Deeds, dating from 1708, up to and including 31st December 1969 are held in paper format. Records from 1st January 1970 to date are held in electronic format. They include:

> land transfers
> marriage settlements
> tenure contracts that are concerned
>   with property transactions.

The full address is:

> The Property Registration Authority, Chancery St, Dublin 7
> Telephone: +353 (0) 1 670 7500
> Email: webmaster@prai.ie
> Website: www.prai.ie

Library of the Representative Church Body

As a result of the fire in the Public Record Office of Ireland in 1922, many Church of Ireland parish registers were lost. The Representative Church Body has gathered together the surviving registers (or copies of them) together with other records relating to the history of the Church of Ireland. The Library now holds some 40,000 printed books, a large and varied collection of pamphlets and a selection of periodicals. Non-current records from parishes, dioceses, cathedrals, the General Synod and the Representative Church Body are regularly transferred to the Library. Copies of those that originated in Northern Ireland have been transferred to the Public Record Office in Belfast, while some records still remain in local custody.

The full address is:
>Library of the Representative Church Body, Braemor Park, Churchtown, Dublin 14
>Telephone: +353 (0) 1 492 3979
>Fax: +353 (0) 1 492 4770
>Website: www.ireland.anglican.org

Library of the Society of Friends

The Society of Friends (Quakers) has a long tradition of philanthropic activity in Ireland. They were involved in providing extensive relief during the Great Famine of 1845-52. Their collection includes both manuscript sources and an extensive library relating to the activities of Quakers in Ireland. They also have a number of genealogical sources. The library only opens on a limited basis. It is worth contacting the librarian before visiting.

The full address is:
>Religious Society of Friends in Ireland, Historical Library, Stocking Lane, Rathfarnham, Dublin 16
>Telephone: +353 (0) 1 495 6890
>Email: qhist@eircom.net
>Website: www.quakers-in-ireland.ie

Military Archives

This office is part of the National Archives. It holds records of the Department of Defence since 1921 and the Defence Forces since 1913. Researchers should write or telephone in advance.

The full address is:

The OC Military Archives, Cathal Brugha Barracks,
Rathmines, Dublin 6
Telephone: +353 (0) 1 497 5499
Fax: +353 (0) 1 497 4027
Website: www.military.ie

Record Depositories in Northern Ireland

Public Record Office of Northern Ireland (PRONI)

This office provides an excellent resource for family historians. Apart from the more obvious genealogical records such as Griffith's *Valuation*, Tithe Applotment books, will calendars and church records, this office also has an excellent collection of:

school registers
business records
emigrants' letters
copies of most pre-1900 registers of baptisms,
    marriages and burials for all denominations in Ulster.

This office also holds some records relating to the historic nine counties of Ulster rather than just the six counties that constitute Northern Ireland. They will carry out specific searches of the records for a fee but are unable to offer a full family tree research service.

The full address is:

The Public Record Office of Northern Ireland
66 Balmoral Avenue, Belfast, BT9 6NY
Telephone: +44 (0) 28 9025 1318
Fax: +44 (0) 28 9025 5999
Email: proni@dcalni.gov.uk
Website: www.proni.gov.uk

N.B. PRONI will be moving to new premises in 2010 or 2011. Check their website for details.

The Registrar-General's Office (General Register Office of Northern Ireland)

This office contains records of the births, deaths and marriages of all people who resided in Northern Ireland after 1921. The records date back to 1864, although registers of non-Catholic marriages began in 1845. Family historians can visit the office although they must book in advance.

The Registrar-General's Office also operates a postal enquiry service. If your ancestor was from Northern Ireland but his or her birth, death or marriage took place before 1921, the appropriate records are kept in the Registrar-General's Office in Dublin (*see above*).

The full address is:

Oxford House, 49-55 Chichester St, Belfast, BT1 4HL
Telephone: +44 (0) 28 9025 2000
Fax: +44 (0) 28 9025 2044
Website: www.groni.gov.uk

Presbyterian Historical Society

The Presbyterian tradition has been strong in the north east region of Ireland since the early 17th century. Some of the oldest surviving registers have been deposited in the Presbyterian Historical Society. Although searchers can visit the Society's premises, they may not be allowed access to the oldest registers. The Public Record Office of Northern Ireland does, however, have copies of these registers on microfilm. The Presbyterian Historical Society does not undertake genealogical searches. The Library is in Room 218 on the second floor and is open Tuesday, Wednesday and Thursday from 10.00am to 12.30pm and from 1.30pm to 4.00pm.

The full address is:

The Presbyterian Historical Society, Church House,
Fisherwick Place, Belfast, BT1 6DW
Telephone: +44 (0) 28 9032 2284
Email: librarian@presbyterianhistoryireland.com
Website: www.presbyterianhistoryireland.com

The Linenhall Library

Nineteen prominent citizens established the Linenhall Library (or The Belfast Library Society for Promoting Knowledge) in 1788. Today, the library holds over 200,000 volumes of books and pamphlets, many of which relate to Irish history. A large part of this collection is of value to the family historian, particularly the Blackwood Pedigrees, a collection of over 1,000 manuscript family trees; an extensive newspaper collection and an index to births, marriages and deaths in the *Belfast News Letter*, covering the years 1738-1864.

The full address is:
  The Linenhall Library, 17 Donegall Square North,
  Belfast, BT1 5GB
  Telephone: +44 (0) 28 9032 1707
  Email: info@linenhall.com
  Website: www.linenhall.com

The Ulster Historical Foundation

The Ulster Historical Foundation was established in 1956 as part of the Public Record Office of Northern Ireland. Although the two organisations were separated in 1988, the Foundation continued to provide a genealogical searching service, and it continues to publish books of genealogical and historical interest. It also has useful online databases, for example;

Virtually all civil marriage records for counties Antrim and Down, as well as a portion of south Armagh (1845-1921)

Virtually all Roman Catholic registers of baptisms and marriages for counties Antrim and Down prior to 1900 (as well as funeral records where they survive)

A large number of Church of Ireland and Presbyterian registers of baptisms and marriages for mid-, south- and west County Down

A large number of Church of Ireland and Presbyterian registers of baptisms and burials for the city of Belfast

Civil birth records for Belfast (incomplete)

Burials in Belfast City Cemetery from 1869 onwards.

The full address is:
> The Ulster Historical Foundation, Unit 7
> Cotton Court, Waring St, Belfast, BT1 2ED
> Telephone: +44 (0) 28 9033 2288
> Website: www.ancestryireland.com

The Irish World Organisation
This organisation has compiled extensive lists of gravestone inscriptions for the counties of Armagh, Londonderry, Fermanagh and Tyrone. It also offers a full range of family history services and has one of Ireland's largest family history databases of church and civil records.

The full address is:
> The Irish World Organisation, 51 Dungannon Road,
> Coalisland, Co. Tyrone, BT71 4HP
> Telephone: +44 (0) 28 8774 6065
> Email: info@irish-world.com
> Website: www.irish-world.com

Most counties in Ireland also possess a family history centre that offers a full genealogical research service. An up-to-date list can be obtained from either the Irish Tourist Board in Dublin or the Northern Ireland Tourist Board.

The addresses you need are:
> Fáilte Ireland, Baggot St Bridge, Dublin 2
> Telephone: +353 (0) 1 602 4000
> Fax: +353 (0) 1 602 4100
> Website: www.discoverireland.ie

> Belfast Welcome Centre / Northern Ireland Tourist Board
> 47 Donegall Place, Belfast BT1 5AD
> Telephone: +44 (0) 28 9024 6609
> Website: wwwdiscovernorthernireland.com /
> www.gotobelfast.com

Record Depositories in London

The National Archives
The National Archives (previously the Public Record Office) contains many record collections and databases relating to Ireland, especially for the period following the creation of the United Kingdom in 1800. A number are useful for family historians, notably records relating to the British Army and the Royal Air Force (both of which included many Irish-born men). The records of the Royal Irish Constabulary include service and disbandment registers. More unusual collections include records relating to the 1916 rebellion and the internment of Irish prisoners in England between 1916 and 1919.

The full address is:
> The National Archives, Ruskin Avenue,
> Kew, Richmond, Surrey, TW9 4DU
> Telephone: +44 (0) 20 8876 3444
> Minicom: +44 (0) 20 8392 9198
> Website: www.nationalarchives.gov.uk

Irish Genealogical Research Society
The Society, founded in 1936, has an active programme for the acquisition of manuscripts and printed works relating to Irish births, marriages and deaths up to 1864, and the collection of copies of wills. Open Saturday afternoons between 2.00pm and 6.00pm. Visit the website for membership details and further information. The Society's Library is located at the Church of St Magnus the Martyr, Lower Thames St, London EC3 6DN. There is an annual publication: *The Irish Genealogist*.

The full address is:
> The Secretary, The Irish Genealogical Research Society
> 18 Stratford Avenue, Rainham, Gillingham, Kent,
> ME8 0EP, England
> Email: info@igrsoc.org
> Website: www.igrsoc.org

Information Sources:
The 20th Century

Civil Registration of Births, Deaths and Marriages

When you have obtained as much background information as possible within the home and in your local library, the next stage is to begin to search the official records. The most useful place to start is in the registers of births, deaths and marriages. These records, apart from providing the 'vital statistics' necessary for any search, also provide valuable leads that will enable you to continue the search in other records.

Civil registration (that is, compulsory registration by the State of births, deaths and marriages) did not commence in Ireland until January 1864. The only exceptions are non-Catholic marriages, which were registered from 1845. The existence of these records means that it is possible to obtain details of the birth, death and marriage of any person in any part of Ireland from 1864 to the present day. It is, therefore, possible to start a search by obtaining a copy of your own birth certificate, then your parents' marriage- and birth certificates, your grandparents' marriage certificate and so on. Thus, these records provide an important and direct link between yourself and your ancestors in the 19th century. Your genealogical search should begin in this way.

The records of births, deaths and marriages are divided into indexes and certificates. You need to locate your ancestor in the index before obtaining a copy of the appropriate certificate.

Indexes

These are arranged according to birth, death or marriage. Each category is subdivided into years. After 1878, the years were further subdivided into quarters – January to March, April to June, July to September, and October to December. Each year is contained within a separate volume, and within each volume the event is registered by name and by its location as defined by Poor Law Union. The number given after the name and location refers to the volume and page number in which the certificate will be found. Marriages are listed in the indexes under the names of both parties. The death indexes also provide the age of each person at death, which is particularly useful if two people with the same name died in the same year. The following are typical sections from the birth and death indexes.

Section of birth index:

Name	Location	Volume	Page No.
Cousens, George	Magherafelt	1	694
Cousens, John	Rathdrum	3	249
Cousins, Mary	Dublin South	1	232
Cousins, Sarah	Dublin North	2	334
Coulter, Hannah	Omagh	1	493

Section of death index:

Name	Age at Death	Location	Volume	Page No.
Murnin, Michael	67	Carrickfergus	3	247
Murphy, Patrick	21	Millstreet	2	301
Murphy, Patrick	75	Cobh	1	129

Birth Certificates

These records contain a great deal of valuable information. They include:

> the given name of the child
> the date and place of birth
> the names of the parents
> the maiden name of the mother
> the occupation of the father
> the parents' address
> the name of the person who registered the birth.

Apart from the obvious value of this information, birth certificates will direct you towards other records. For example, when you know the names of both parents, it will make it easier to locate their marriage certificate. It is generally safe to assume that the marriage took place within a few years of the first child being born. The address from a birth certificate is particularly valuable because it will help you to search other records such as census returns or parish registers.

Marriage Certificates
These certificates are usually the easiest to locate because they are listed in the indexes under both the bride's name and groom's name. They provide:

> the name of the parish
> the Poor Law Union and the county in which the
>   marriage took place
> the church or office where the ceremony was performed
> the date of the marriage
> the full names of the bride and groom
> their ages – although this frequently only states 'of
>   full age', which means over 21
> the marital status of both parties (bachelor,
>   spinster, widow etc.)
> the occupation, rank or profession of both parties
> their addresses
> the names and occupations of the fathers of
>   both the bride and groom (even if they were dead)
> the names of the witnesses.

The marriage certificate will also give you the opportunity to see your ancestors' signatures, although some certificates are signed with an 'X' ('their mark' which generally denotes that they were unable to write). For family historians, the marriage certificate provides a wide range of useful information. If, for example, the age is provided, it will make it easier to search for the birth certificates of both parties as well as for any offspring. Details about the fathers of the bride and groom can take the search back one generation.

Death Certificates
Although these certificates are generally regarded as containing the least valuable information for family historians, they are still worth consulting. Death certificates provide:

the age of the deceased person (although this
    is sometimes a guess and may not be accurate)
where the deceased died (this may be a hospital or
    a workhouse)
the former occupation of the deceased. In the case of
    a young child, the name of the parents is generally
    recorded instead of occupation
the cause of death
the name of the informant and his or her relationship
    to the deceased (in most cases the informant was
    a relative of the deceased person).

Although the age stated on a death certificate could
sometimes be inaccurate, it will provide an approximate
guide to when the deceased person was born. This, in turn,
will enable you to search for a birth certificate. It is interesting
to note that the cause of death, especially in the 19th century,
was frequently attributed to 'old age' or 'general decline'.

Where to find these records
Records for the period before 1922 for the whole of Ireland
are held in Dublin at the General Register Office, Government
Offices, Convent Road, Roscommon.

After 1922, the records are divided between offices in
Dublin and Belfast depending on whether the event took
place in the Republic of Ireland or Northern Ireland. The
address in Northern Ireland is General Register Office of
Northern Ireland, Oxford House, 49-55 Chichester St, Belfast
BT1 4HL.

Both offices are open to the public and they both operate
a postal enquiry service. Before visiting these offices, find
out their hours and days of opening, current fees and the
availability of the records to the public by checking their
websites.

A valuable resource has been provided by The Church
of Jesus Christ of Latter-Day Saints (the Mormons) who
have made microfilm copies of the early registers of births,

deaths and marriages for all of Ireland (and, in fact, most of the world). Inquiries should be made to the Family History Centre, c/o The Willows, Finglas Road, Glasnevin, Dublin 11, or the Family History Centre, 403 Holywood Road, Belfast, BT4 2GU.

Researchers can use these offices, although opening hours are restricted.

When searching any of the above records, it is worth bearing in mind the following points:

1. Before you visit a Record Office, find as much background information as possible about each person being searched, particularly names, approximate dates and locations. The local Poor Law Union is the most useful unit of address.
2. Always check for all surname variants in the records.
3. Allow some latitude in searching for any given year, as ages are often approximate. Remember that the index will refer to the date that an event was registered and not when it occurred. For example, if a child was born in December 1889, he or she may not appear in the indexes until January or February 1890.
4. Always check the back of each index for miscellaneous entries such as 'births at sea', 'deaths during the Boer War', 'late entries' etc.
5. If you are looking for an ancestor about whom not much is known, it may be worth making a note of all the possible entries in the indexes. However, do not assume that anyone with the same surname as your ancestor is necessarily related.
6. Occasionally, a person may not be located in the indexes. This may be because a few people – either deliberately or otherwise – slipped through the administrative net particularly in the early years of civil registration. If this happens, concentrate instead on the other sources that are available.

Census Returns

Census returns are a rich source of information in any genealogical search. Not only do they provide valuable insights into the ancestors you already know of, they also frequently bring to light ancestors of whom you may have been unaware.

The first government census for the entire Irish population was taken in 1821, with additional censuses being taken every ten years from 1831 to 1911. No census was taken in 1921, although censuses were taken independently in 1926 in both the newly created Free State (which later became the Republic of Ireland) and Northern Ireland.

Unfortunately, for both historians and genealogists, only fragments of the 19th-century census returns have survived. The returns for the years 1821, 1831, 1841 and 1851, which were deposited in the Public Record Office in Dublin, were almost totally destroyed by fire in 1922. The 1861, 1871, 1881 and 1891 returns fared little better; even before the fire of 1922 they had been destroyed by government order. Some of them were, in fact, pulped for the 'war effort' during 1914-18.

As a result of the turbulent history of Irish census records, the 1901 census is the earliest complete return to survive for the whole country. The 1911 census has also survived and both of these censuses are now available for consultation in the National Archives in Dublin. The 1901 census for Northern Ireland is available on microfilm in the Public Record Office of Northern Ireland. The availability of the 1901 and 1911 census returns places an enormous fund of information at the disposal of family historians.

The National Archives of Ireland, in conjunction with the Library and Archives Canada, is undertaking a digitisation programme of both censuses. The first phase of the Irish 1901 and 1911 census website, containing the records for Dublin 1911, fully indexed by name, and with free access to the digitised images of the original manuscript household forms, was launched in December 2007. The site also contains a wealth of photographs and essays on life on Dublin at that time, with links to illustrative census forms. The second phase, the records for counties Antrim, Down and Kerry, was launched in December 2008, with other counties to follow in due course. More details are available on their website: www. census.nationalarchives.ie.

All censuses taken after 1921, in both Northern Ireland and the Republic of Ireland, are subject to a 100-year closure rule, which means they will not be available for public consultation for some years.

The purpose of collecting censuses was to provide the central government with information about the population. However, by recording details about age, family relationships, literacy, marital status, place of origin, etc., they provide a unique insight into family life at the turn of the century. The 1901 census is particularly valuable because it provides a link between the 20th- and 19th centuries. Also, apart from the intrinsic value of the information provided in a census return, it can help to direct you to other sources of information.

To find an ancestor in the 1901 or 1911 census, you only need to know his or her address at the time the census was taken. If he resided in a town, his street address is necessary. If she lived in the countryside, the townland address is required. A search in the birth, death and marriage records will provide the addresses. These can be corroborated by either a search in a street directory, or the Annual Revision Lists of Griffith's *Valuation*.

The 1901 and 1911 censuses are arranged by household. Each member of the household is listed, as well as family, servants and any visitors to the house on the night that the census was taken. If your ancestor does not appear on the list with the rest of the family, it could be because they were staying with a relative, or were working as a servant, and will be included in that family's census returns.

Detailed information is provided on each member of the household, such as:

relationship to the head of the household

age
occupation
religion
ability to read and write
marital status
ability to speak Irish
county of birth
any physical or mental handicaps.

The information provided in the censuses can be used in a variety of ways. For example, the inclusion of age will enable you to estimate when a person was born. If he or she was born after 1864, the birth certificate can then be located in the registers of births, deaths and marriages. The ages provided should, however, only be used as a rough guide to the actual date of birth. A comparison between the ages given in the 1901 census with those given in the 1911 census often shows more than a 10-year age discrepancy.

The census returns also provide a description of the dwelling place of each household. This, together with the details of occupation and servants (if any) residing in the house, will provide a clearer understanding of the social and economic status of your ancestor. Inclusion of the county of birth can be particularly useful as it will allow you to follow the movements of your ancestors. This is helpful in the case of large cities such as Belfast and Dublin that grew rapidly in the late 19th century, mainly as a result of migration from the countryside. It is interesting to note that in the 1911 census, married women were required to state how long they had been married and how many children had been born to the family, either dead or alive. Thus the date of marriage can be established and a marriage certificate located in the appropriate registry office.

Some fragments of the early 19th-century censuses have survived and they are available in both the National Archives in Dublin and the Public Record Office of Northern Ireland. The early census returns do not contain as much detailed information as the later ones but, where they exist, they are worth consulting. The 1841 census, for example, gave details on absent members of the family, including those who had died or emigrated in the previous ten years.

The loss of the 19th-century records is partly compensated for by the existence of Old Age Pension claims. When the Old Age Pension Act was introduced in 1909, the 1841 and 1851 censuses were searched in order to establish the true ages of those people claiming benefit. The results of these searches are now held in the National Archives and the Public Record Office of Northern Ireland. These are particularly valuable in helping to locate an ancestor's age and address in the middle of the 19th century.

Census returns, therefore, provide useful and fascinating information about each family and each individual who resided in Ireland in 1901 and 1911. Consult them at an early stage in your search. These returns, and any earlier ones which survive, will provide a solid foundation of information to take your search back to the 19th century and, in some cases, even earlier.

Old Age Pension Returns
The Old Age Pension Act was introduced in Ireland in 1909. This legislation meant that for the first time people over a certain age (initially 70) and 'of good character' were guaranteed a payment from the State (a pension). However, because the compulsory registration of births had only started in 1864, claimants of the pension were unable to provide the government with a copy of their birth certificates. The government, therefore, attempted to establish a person's date of birth by allowing a search to be made of the census returns for 1841 and 1851.

These searches were carried out in two ways. In return for a small fee, claimants could provide information that could be used to locate their family in the early census returns. Claimants who were found in these returns were then given a certified copy of the relevant census. These certified copies are now held in the National Archives in Dublin (formerly the Public Record Office of Ireland) and the Public Record Office of Northern Ireland. Claimants who applied for their pension through their local pension office had to fill in a Form 37. This form was sent to the Public Record Office in Dublin to enable a search in the relevant census returns to be made. When the search was completed, comments such as 'family found', 'claimant 3 years old in 1841' or 'family not found' were added to the form. Moreover, in the case of a dispute, the forms were used to record the names, ages, relationships and, sometimes, occupations of the entire family.

Again, the surviving Form 37s are divided between the National Archives in Dublin (for the twenty-six counties) and Public Record Office in Belfast (for the six counties in Northern Ireland).

The unique value of these Old Age Pension returns lies in the fact that they refer to information no longer available due to the destruction of the 19th-century census returns. Unfortunately, these records are not indexed and it can take a long time to locate an entry for any particular family. They are, however, grouped by county, and it is worth searching through these county volumes as they contain vital information on age, family relationships and where the family resided. This, in turn, will enable you to make a search of other 19th-century records.

Information Sources:
The 19th Century

Griffith's *Valuation* and Tithe Applotment Books

As we have seen, census returns are an extremely valuable source for family research. It is unfortunate that so few survive for the 19th century. However, other contemporary records may contain the required information. For the 19th century, two collections of records exist that have come to be regarded as census substitutes. They are Griffith's *Valuation*, which covers the period 1848–64, and the Tithe Applotment Books, compiled between 1823 and 1838. Despite their odd sounding names, these sources are extremely useful and they should be consulted by all family historians at some stage during their search.

The usefulness of Griffith's *Valuation* and the Tithe Applotment Books lies in the fact that they cover the period before civil registration began. A county-by-county index provides a short cut to using these records. Its title is *An Index to the Surnames of Householders in Griffith's Primary Valuation* and the *Tithe Applotment Books*, but it is more usually referred to as *The Householder's Index*. Copies are available in the principal Record Offices in Dublin and Belfast and in county libraries and family history centres.

Griffith's *Valuation*

Griffith's *Valuation* was a survey of all land in Ireland. It was carried out for the purpose of determining the amount of rates (local taxes) to be paid by each occupier through the assessment of the value of their property. The *Valuation* was named after Richard Griffith, the geologist and engineer who was responsible for the survey.

Griffith's *Valuation* is a goldmine for family historians whose ancestors occupied land (both rented or owned) between 1848 and 1864. The first *Valuation* was carried out for County Dublin in l848, and the final one for County Armagh in 1864. The results of the completed *Valuation* were then printed and published. Copies of the *Valuation* are now available widely in libraries, family history centres and Record Offices.

Griffith's *Valuation* is arranged by county, Poor Law Union, parish and townland. To find an ancestor in the *Valuation*, you need to know the name of the head of the household at the time that the survey was carried out and the name of the townland, parish and Poor Law Union in which he or she occupied property. The *Townland Index* will give you the name of the relevant Union and parish.

Suppose you are looking for a Matthew Morrison who resided in the parish of Clones in the Poor Law Union of Irvine in County Fermanagh. You must locate the relevant county volume and then the relevant entry under Union, parish and townland. The record might show that a Richard Morrison occupied a house, office ('office' usually refers to barns, dairies, cowsheds, etc.) and land, valued at £8 5s 0d which he rented from an Adam McCullough, 'the immediate lessor' or landlord. Within the same parish you might find a Jeremiah Morrison who could be a relative. It might be worth making a note of all people with the same name in the parish.

Griffith's *Valuation* was carried out with the purpose of levying rates and it is primarily concerned with land – its size, quality and value. This information is a good indication of the economic standing of your ancestors. The valuation record also includes a reference number in the left hand corner that corresponds to a number on the *Ordnance Survey Townland Maps*. This will enable you to locate the property and, if you are fortunate, the building may still be standing, although don't be too disappointed if you find it is now used as a cowshed!

The government required that a record of all changes in occupancy should be kept and so subsequent changes in landholders can be traced using the Rate Revision Books, available from *c.* 1870 up to approximately 1930. This can be both useful and fascinating. If, for example, you have located Matthew Morrison in Griffith's *Valuation* you can follow the progress of his piece of land. If the Revision Books showed that the land changed hands in 1890, perhaps Matthew died (look, then, for a death certificate and will), or perhaps emigrated. The Frederick Morrison who took over the land was probably Matthew's eldest son or possibly a younger brother.

In conclusion, Griffith's *Valuation* will enable you to pinpoint where your ancestor resided in the middle of the 19th century and also help you to gauge his or her economic standing. It will further allow you to follow the history of the property up to about 1930. Both the printed valuation and the rate revisions for Northern Ireland are available in the Public Record Office of Northern Ireland in Belfast. For researchers with ancestors who resided in the Republic of Ireland, Griffith's *Valuation* is available in the National Archives, Dublin, and the Revaluation Books (sometimes referred to as Revision Books) are located at the Valuation Office, Irish Life Centre, Abbey St Lower, Dublin 1.

1830 Valuation
In 1830 a valuation was carried out to list people who occupied property in Ireland. This valuation is not as complete as the one carried out by Richard Griffith (Griffith's *Valuation*) after 1848. Only relatively few households are included and they tend to be the highest rated properties. If you locate your ancestor in Griffith's *Valuation*, it is worth checking to see if your ancestor was also mentioned in the 1830 valuation.

Revaluation Books, 1848-1929
Following the completion of Griffith's *Valuation*, each local valuation office was obliged to update the information on land occupancy as necessary. This took the form of noting:

a change in the occupier and immediate lessor (landlord)
the date the change took place.

Because a change in tenancy often signified a death, you should always make a search for a death certificate and a search in the will calendars. The Revaluation Books can also be used to confirm the address of an ancestor at the beginning of the 20th century and consequently can facilitate a search being made in the census returns.

The Revaluation Books are arranged according to townlands that are, in turn, grouped into electoral divisions. The name of the appropriate electoral divisions can be obtained from the *Townland Index*. The Revaluation Books are available for public consultation. In the Republic of Ireland they are available in the General Valuation Office in Dublin, and in Northern Ireland at the Public Record Office in Belfast.

Tithe Applotment Books

If you are successful in locating your ancestors in Griffith's *Valuation*, then the next step back into the past is to consult the Tithe Applotment Books. This record will enable you to see if your family had lived in the same place thirty or forty years earlier.

The tithe was a form of tax paid by people of all denominations for the purpose of maintaining the Church of Ireland, which was the Established, or State Church until 1869. Originally the tithe was paid 'in kind'. However, an Act passed in 1823 required it to be paid in cash. In order to bring about this change, all agricultural land in Ireland had to be surveyed and valued (apploted). This investigation was carried out by local surveyors between 1823 and 1837.

The tithe had to be paid by all occupiers of land within the country, the only exceptions being church lands, glebes (land occupied by clergymen) and urban areas. Because the money raised was used for the upkeep of the Church of Ireland, this tax was disliked by people of other religious persuasions, who formed the majority of the population at that time. In the 1830s, this resentment resulted in an outbreak of agrarian protest (referred to as 'outrages') that became known as the 'tithe war'. As a consequence of this unrest, tithes were virtually abolished in 1838 when they were reduced in amount and landlords rather than tenants were made responsible for their payment.

The tithe survey was divided into civil parishes which were subdivided into townlands. In order to determine how much tithe should be paid, the surveyors assessed the average income that could be expected from each piece of land or farm. The results of this survey were compiled into the Tithe Applotment Books. Like Griffith's *Valuation*, they will tell you about the quantity and quality of land occupied by your ancestors.

The Tithe Applotment Books comprise over 2,000 handwritten volumes. Although they vary slightly in quality, they all provide the same basic information. The Tithe Applotment Books are not comprehensive because they do not include either people who lived in towns or landless labourers. They do, however, provide the first register of all landholders in Ireland. The information contained in the Tithe Applotment Books is particularly important due to the destruction of the early 19th-century censuses. They are, in fact, the most comprehensive lists of rural dwellings that exist for the period before the Famine and are therefore generally regarded as an early census substitute.

The Tithe Applotment Books are available for the twenty-six counties at the National Archives in Dublin and for the six counties of Northern Ireland at the Public Record Office in Belfast. A surname index which lists all the surnames mentioned in the Tithe Applotment Books and Griffith's *Valuation* is available in major libraries and Record Offices. The surnames are listed alphabetically under county divisions. This index makes the searching process easier. If your ancestor's surname (or any variant of it) does not appear in the index, then there is little point in searching in either Griffith's *Valuation* or the Tithe Applotment Books.

Landed Estates: Court Rentals, *c.* 1850-1885

During the Great Famine of 1845-52, a great deal of land changed hands in Ireland. Many poor tenants (almost 500,000 out of a population of 8,500,000 people in 1841) were legally evicted from their holdings. Illegal evictions were also commonplace. Additionally, during these years a large number of landlords sold their estates, unable – or unwilling – to pay the spiralling Poor Rates levied for the provision of poor relief (usually in the local workhouse).

The sale of property, especially when owned by absentee or indebted landlords, was encouraged by the British government who introduced legislation known as the Encumbered Estates Acts in 1848 and 1849. Brochures, known as 'rentals', were issued before the sale of property through the courts and these provided detailed information on each property being sold. These brochures or rentals generally include lists of tenants, details of rents paid, conditions of tenure, etc.

An important collection known as the O'Brien Set of Encumbered/Landed Estates Court Rentals is held in the National Archives in Dublin.

Parish Registers

Parish registers are an invaluable source for family historians for the period prior to 1864 (before the registration of births, deaths and marriages was made compulsory). Unfortunately, due to neglect, accidental destruction or government repression, many of these records only start during the 19th century. The Penal Laws, for example, in force between 1692 and 1793, restricted the ability of non-conformist denominations (including Catholics and Presbyterians) to practise their religion openly.

Parish registers provide valuable information on baptisms, marriages and burials. In order to use them effectively you need to know:

the area in which your ancestor lived
his or her religious denomination
the approximate date of the event (i.e. the
    baptism, marriage or burial).

Remember, however, that before compulsory State registration, this information was recorded voluntarily in local church registers and may be incomplete or inaccurate. Widespread illiteracy at the time means that the spelling of a surname or townland can vary with each member of the same family.

The age of parish registers varies from parish to parish although, due to intermittent periods of repression, the oldest records tend to be those of the Church of Ireland. Parish registers vary greatly in the extent of information they provide, but generally include the details listed below.

Baptisms
Information on the baptism included:
> name of child
> date and location of event
> date of birth (occasionally)
> parents' names, including maiden name of mother. (In the case of illegitimate children the putative father is frequently named)
> parents' address (occasionally, provided by townland)
> parents' occupation
> names of sponsors (generally only in Catholic ceremonies)
> name of minister performing the ceremony.

Marriages
Information on the marriage included:
> name of bride and groom
> their places of residence
> date and location of marriage (possibly in the bride's home)
> names of witnesses.

Burials
Records relating to burials are rare, especially those relating to Catholic and Presbyterian burials. Burial records include:
> name and residence of the deceased
> burial date and place

the age of the deceased (occasionally). In the case of young children, the names of the parents are generally included.

Using Parish Records

Although parish registers are an extremely fruitful source of information, they can be difficult to use. They are not generally indexed, so searching through a register can be very time consuming. This is particularly true where the handwriting and layout is haphazard. Parish registers are also scattered and, apart from the early Church of Ireland registers, are not public documents. It might be necessary to obtain permission to consult them. Most indexes and official records are arranged according to civil parish. These can differ slightly from the parish areas covered by the main denominations. Take care to relate parishes to their appropriate church district.

Apart from information relating to baptisms, marriages and burials, parish registers can also include a great deal of miscellaneous information relating to people and events in the parish. A number of excellent parish histories have been written and they should be consulted where possible. Your local library should be able to advise you as to their availability.

The three main Christian denominations in Ireland are Roman Catholic, Church of Ireland and Presbyterian. Each of these denominations produces a directory that is updated annually and provides the name and address of each church and its current incumbent. The information is particularly useful if the parish register in which you are interested is still in local custody.

Church of Ireland Records

The Church of Ireland is variously known as the Anglican, Established, Episcopalian or State Church. From the 16th to the 19th centuries, this Church was the State Church in Ireland despite the fact that throughout this period the majority of people in Ireland were Roman Catholics. In 1869, the Church of Ireland was disestablished and consequently ceased to be the State Church. After this date, the registers of the Church of Ireland became public records and were deposited in the Public Record Office in Dublin. By 1922, the records of over 1,000 parishes had been deposited. Unfortunately, in that year approximately two-thirds of these records were lost as a consequence of the fire in the Public Record Office during the course of the Irish Civil War (1922-23). Luckily, about one-third of the local parish churches had either retained their registers or made copies of them before sending them to Dublin. Moreover, the registers of thirty of the oldest parishes were being transcribed at the time by the Parish Register Society and consequently they were also saved.

The main repository for all surviving Church of Ireland records is:

> The Representative Church Body, Braemor Park,
> Churchtown, Dublin 14
> Telephone: +353 (0) 1 492 3979

It is advisable to contact this office before visiting. The Public Record Office of Northern Ireland has copies of most of the surviving Church of Ireland registers for the nine counties of Ulster on microfilm.

It is worth noting that even if your ancestor did not belong to the Church of Ireland, restrictions on his or her own religious practices may have resulted in him or her using this Church to perform important ceremonies. Therefore, when looking for an ancestor of any denomination, it is worthwhile searching the registers of the local Anglican Church.

Presbyterian Records

The Presbyterian Church in Ireland was established in Ulster during the early 17th century by Scottish settlers (also known as *planters*). A number of Presbyterian ministers followed these settlers. In 1642, a presbytery was established in Ulster by chaplains of a Scottish army who had been sent to Ireland to crush an uprising by Catholics in 1641. Since that time, the strongest base of support of Presbyterianism has been in the north-eastern part of the country. King William III (William of Orange) rewarded Presbyterian support in his war against the Catholic king, James II, by increasing financial support to the Church.

The earliest Presbyterian registers relate to Antrim town in County Antrim and date back to 1674. These registers are unique as the majority of Presbyterian registers only start in the early 19th century. Presbyterian records began relatively late because during the 17th and 18th centuries Presbyterians, in common with other non-conformist or 'dissenter' religions, were subject to various restrictions regarding the way they could practise their religion. In 1661, for example, all Presbyterian ministers were required to swear assent to the Church of Ireland's *Book of Common Prayer*. When sixty-one of the sixty-eight ministers refused to do so, they were subsequently deposed from their ministries. Although these restrictions were enforced only sporadically, Presbyterians could only be legally married or buried according to the rites of the Church of Ireland.

A number of Presbyterians, especially if they owned property, paid nominal allegiance to the Church of Ireland for the purpose of 'legitimising' their heirs. In 1719, the Toleration Act gave Presbyterians more freedom to practise their religion. It was not until 1782, however, that Presbyterian marriages were officially recognised by the State, although marriages between a Presbyterian and a member of another faith were not made legal until 1844. With these and other restrictions it is not surprising that the majority of Presbyterian registers did not start until the 19th century. Fortunately, other early church records survive, relating to the various Presbyterian congregations in Ireland. The most common are the Session Minute Books or the Kirk Session Minutes. They were usually kept by the Elders (ministers) of each congregation and contained a variety of information, such as details of:

recent arrivals in the area
new communicants
details of baptisms and marriages within
    the congregation
names of emigrants.

Where these records have survived, they can provide a greater depth of information than ordinary parish registers.

Some of the oldest parish registers and Session Minute Books have been deposited in the Presbyterian Historical Society, Spires Centre, Fisherwick Place, Belfast BT1 6DW.

While not all of these records are available for public consultation, the Public Record Office of Northern Ireland has either the originals, or copies, of many Presbyterian registers relating to the nine counties of Ulster. The Record Office also has a Guide to Church Records that provides details of all of the churches for which it holds records. A number of records are still in local custody and you may need permission from the relevant minister in order to consult them.

Useful information about the Presbyterian Church can be found in the following books:
    Margaret Dickson Falley, *Irish and Scotch-Irish
        Ancestral Research* (reprinted 1995)
    Finlay Holmes, *Our Irish Presbyterian Heritage* (1992)
    W.D. Killen, *History of Congregations of the Presbyterian
        Church in Ireland and Biographical Notices of
        Eminent Presbyterian Ministers and Laymen* (1886)
    The Presbyterian Historical Society, *A History
        of Congregations in the Presbyterian Church in
        Ireland 1610-1982* (1982).

Non-Subscribing Presbyterian Records

The Presbyterian Church in Ireland has undergone many rifts and internal divisions, most notably in the 18th and early 19th centuries. The Public Record Office of Northern Ireland has either the originals or copies of the surviving Non-Subscribing Presbyterian registers.

Methodist Records

Methodism began as a religious movement within the Established Church through the efforts of John and Charles Wesley in the 18th century. It was characterised by evangelical theology, lay preaching and an informal church structure (preaching in fields was very common). The extension of Methodism to Ireland pre-dated John Wesley's first visit to the country in 1747, but its influence spread more rapidly after the 1750s. Yet Methodism never achieved a growth in Ireland comparable to its successes elsewhere.

The formal records of the Methodist Church did not begin until the late 19th century. Until that time, many Methodists did not keep their own registers but were baptised and married according to the rites of the Church of Ireland. The Public Record Office of Northern Ireland has the most complete collection of Methodist records, details of which can be found in their Guide to Church Records.

Quaker Records

The Society of Friends, or Quakers, has always been noted for their excellence in record keeping, and their church registers are no exception. These records survive from the late 17th century when Quakers first appeared in Ireland.

The records for the Republic of Ireland are held at The Religious Society of Friends, Quaker House, Stocking Lane, Rathfarnham, Dublin 16.

The records for Northern Ireland are deposited in The Religious Society of Friends, 7 Railway Cottages, Lambeg, Lisburn, Co. Antrim BT27 4QW.

The Public Record Office of Northern Ireland also has copies of many of their church registers.

An excellent guide to Quaker records has been compiled by Olive C. Goodbody, entitled *A Guide to Irish Quaker Records*. It is published by the Irish Manuscripts Commission (now part of the National Library).

Throughout their history, the Quakers have also been admired for their philanthropic activities. Their involvement in providing relief during the Great Famine has been described in *A Suitable Channel: Quaker Relief in the Great Famine* by Rob Goodbody (1995).

Huguenot Records

Huguenots were French Protestants who settled in Ireland in the latter part of the 17th century after escaping religious persecution in their own country. They settled primarily in Portarlington, Youghal, Waterford, Cork, Lisburn and Dublin, and brought with them their own distinctive surnames such as D'Ollior, Fontaine and La Touche. At the beginning of the 20th century, their church records and archives were deposited in the Public Record Office (now the National Archives, Ireland) in Dublin. Fortunately, many of them had been transcribed by the Huguenot Society in London before the fire in the Record Office destroyed the originals in 1922. The Huguenot records survive in published form.

Jewish Records

Jewish people have a long, although not continuous, history in Ireland. Some of the early references date back to the 11th century although it is not until the 17th century that Jews appear consistently in the records. By 1700, Dublin had a rabbi and in 1718, a Jewish cemetery was opened. There was also at this time an organised Jewish community in Cork. Numbers, however, remained small. The Irish census for 1861 registered only 393 Jews and this had fallen to 285 by 1871. However, many Jewish immigrants from eastern Europe arrived in Ireland at the end of the 19th century to escape religious persecution. By 1901, Jewish numbers had risen to 3,769. The Jewish population in Ireland has declined during the 20th century.

Records for the Jewish community are held in The Irish Jewish Museum, 3-4 Walworth Road, South Circular Road, Dublin.

A history of their settlement in Ireland can be found in *A Short History of the Jews in Ireland* by B. Shillman (1943) and *The Jews in Ireland* by Louis Hyman (1972).

Roman Catholic Records

Between the 1690s and 1829, the Roman Catholic Church in Ireland was subject to various legislative restrictions by the government, despite the fact that it was the church of approximately eighty per cent of the population. As a consequence of these restrictions, it was illegal for Roman Catholic men to train for the priesthood, vote in elections or sit in parliament, or for priests to celebrate mass. From the 1770s, these restrictions were gradually removed, although it was not until the passing of the Catholic Emancipation Act of 1829 that Catholics could finally sit in parliament. Because of this repression, many Catholic Church registers do not start until the beginning of the 19th century or until after 1829, the year the Catholic Emancipation Act was passed.

The way information was recorded in Catholic parish registers varied greatly. The entries were sometimes written in Latin and the most commonly encountered words are:

    baptisatus (baptised)
    matrionio (married)
    septulus (buried)
    mater (mother)
    pater (father)
    die (day)
    sponsores (sponsors)
    bannis (banns).

Because Catholic registers are not State records, they are still in local custody and it may be necessary to obtain the permission of the local priest or bishop in order to consult them. The National Library of Ireland has microfilm copies of all registers up to 1880 but, again, permission may be required to consult some of them. The Public Record Office of Northern Ireland has copies of Catholic registers for the nine counties of Ulster and details of this collection can be obtained from their Guide to Church Records.

Gravestone Inscriptions

In Ireland the practice of erecting a headstone to mark the position of a grave is relatively recent, for the most part only dating back to the 17th century. For the family historian, the survival of such a headstone, particularly for the period before 1864, may be the only tangible proof of the existence of an elusive ancestor.

Gravestone inscriptions can provide a surprisingly wide variety of information. In addition to details on an individual ancestor, such as date of birth or age at death, they can show family networks, such as 'beloved daughter of…', or 'adored wife of…'. In some cases, they can reveal names of earlier generations of ancestors. Other miscellaneous information found on gravestones can include:

  address
  occupation
  cause of death
  place of birth (especially in the case of immigrants)
  personal attributes of the deceased.

The type of gravestone erected also gives an insight into the economic and social status of the family.

Most people were buried in the area in which they lived. If you know where your ancestor was buried, you may decide to visit the graveyard. If you do, remember to take a pen and paper – and possibly boots. A camera will also allow you to make a permanent record of the gravestone. If the headstone is overgrown or covered with lichen, you should not attempt to clear it without expert advice. Inscriptions that are difficult to read can be highlighted with chalk. 'Grave rubbings' are also a good way of recovering information.

Because a graveyard may contain a few hundred headstones, some of them old or barely legible, you should, whenever possible, use any published recordings which may exist. The work of transcribing gravestones is not recent. At the end of the 19th century, the Association for the Preservation of the Memorials of the Dead began to record gravestone inscriptions. Unfortunately, they carried out this work sporadically and tended to copy what they considered to be the most interesting headstones. Their recordings have been published and from this source it is possible to gauge how many gravestones have disappeared, even within the last hundred years. The work of transcribing gravestones in Ireland is still continuing: R.J. Clarke published a series for gravestones in counties Antrim and Down, and many local history societies have published details of cemeteries in their areas. These are available for consultation in libraries and family history centres. You should ask in these offices for details of what other published sources are available in the locality.

Wills

When you have located an ancestor and established his or her date of death, the next step in the genealogical search is to establish whether they left a will. Once probated, a will becomes a matter of public record and is available to the public at the Probate Office. The purpose of the probate was to establish officially the authenticity of a will. After about six years, the wills are transferred to the Public Record Offices.

Many family historians tend to think it unlikely that their ancestors would have had sufficient wealth to leave a will. This widely held belief is not true. A surprisingly large number of people in the 18th- and 19th centuries did leave wills even if, by our standards, the amount of money or property tends to be small. It is worth bearing in mind that even if your immediate ancestor did not leave a will, it is possible that a great-great aunt or uncle may have named your ancestor in theirs.

Wills are a particularly rich source for the family historian as they usually provide detailed information about family relationships and are clear indicators of the economic and social status of the deceased. They may also provide a rare insight into the dead person's character – for example, 'I leave my house and its contents, farm and new buckskin trousers to my second son John, more commonly known as 'Jack'. I leave nothing to my first son, Henry.' But while a number of personal details might be included, the fact that a will is also a legal and, ultimately, a public document, means that the terms of a will are usually stated clearly and precisely.

The process of making a will often appears to be complicated and shrouded in mysterious legal jargon. The language used has changed little over the last five hundred years. The person who makes a will is known as a *testator* if a man, or a *testatrix* if a woman. Apart from his or her name, the will includes the names of the executors, who are responsible for seeing that the instructions are carried out, and those of the witnesses. In the 19th century, both witnesses and executors tended to be related to the testator.

The date when the will was drawn up and witnessed will be included on the document. Sometimes a will might have been drawn up many years before the death of the testator. If, during this period, the testator decided to change his will, it was done by adding a codicil to the original. A *codicil* is simply a supplement that modifies or revokes one of the will's provisions. It may reflect a change of fortune, a change of heart (for example, a son may have fallen out of favour and been subsequently excluded from a will), or it may indicate new additions or losses to a family.

Generally, wills were probated within twelve months of the testator's death, although longer lapses are not unusual. So, when searching for a will, remember to search for at least ten years after the testator's death.

A person may die leaving no will. This is known as *dying intestate* and when this occurs the law has guidelines as to who should inherit the estate. Usually, in these cases, a close relative can apply for a Letter of Administration which outlines the allocations to be made. Letters of Administration are particularly useful because they provide the names of the next-of-kin of the deceased.

The amount of information contained in each will varies considerably, usually depending on the amount of money and the number of people who are named as beneficiaries. Wills usually span three generations – that is, they often name spouses, children and grandchildren. The really useful thing about wills is that family relationships are often clearly stated, for example, 'to my beloved second wife, Eileen' or 'to my daughters, Henrietta Smith, Bridget Jones and Mary Black'. Apart from the immediate family, wills often include more distant relatives, sometimes even those who had emigrated. The black sheep of the family or an illegitimate child may even be named in a will, perhaps as a final attempt by the deceased to make amends. In this way, a will might bring to your notice many hitherto unknown ancestors.

Married women rarely held property in their own right until the 20th century, so few of them made wills. However, the will of a spinster, a bachelor or childless widower is generally a rich source of genealogical information, because in cases where there was no obvious heir, a wide variety of relatives were likely to be included in the distribution of the largesse. Hence, brothers, sisters, nieces, nephews, cousins and godchildren were beneficiaries. A favoured servant, neighbour or friend might also be mentioned. Between 1536 and 1858 the proving (or probating) of wills was the sole responsibility of the Church of Ireland. During this period, wills were probated in local diocesan courts or, if the land was held in more than one diocese and valued at over £5, the will was probated in the Prerogative Court of the Archbishop of Armagh. The wills of people of all denominations were probated in these courts, including those of Presbyterians and Roman Catholics.

In 1858, Church of Ireland involvement with wills was brought to an end and they came under civil jurisdiction. This was made possible by the establishment of the Court of Probate that had a Principal Registry in Dublin and eleven District Registries, including one in Belfast. Wills, therefore, fall into two main categories:

those probated before 1858 (when the Church of Ireland had responsibility for them)

those probated after 1858 (when the State became responsible).

Will Depositories

Wills that were probated by the Church authorities up to 1858, and those probated in the twelve registries between 1858 and 1900, were deposited in Dublin. Unfortunately, all of the original records were destroyed by fire in 1922. However, either copies or indexes survive for approximately two-thirds of the original wills. Copies of wills probated between 1858 and 1900, kept by the District Registrars, have been deposited in the two principal records offices in Ireland – the National Archives in Dublin and the Public Record Office of Northern Ireland in Belfast. The Abstract of Wills books for the registries of Armagh, Londonderry and Belfast, for the period 1858-1900 have survived and these have been microfilmed by the Public Record Office of Northern Ireland.

The surviving copies of wills from the previous period, however, present more of a problem, as they are scattered in various depositories throughout the country. Locating the appropriate collection can be difficult.

The National Archives in Dublin has an index of over 20,000 entries of pre-1855 wills. It also has a large collection known as the Betham Wills. This collection consists of approximately 42,000 abstracts of wills and administrations collected by Sir William Betham. These wills cover the period 1536-1800 and relate only to people who were wealthy. The National Archives also has copies of wills from the Grove Collection and the Crosslé Collection.

For the period before 1858, the Public Record Office of Northern Ireland has abstracts of approximately 16,000 wills collected by Sir Bernard Burke, a former Ulster King of Arms. The Record Office has compiled an index of approximately 15,000 wills which were scattered in various collections. It also has copies of wills in three main collections named after the compilers – the Groves, Crosslé and Leslie collections.

Calendars of Wills
For the period after 1858, calendars of wills (printed annually) are available. These are known as the Irish Will Calendars and they are available in the main Record Offices. The Calendars were compiled on a yearly basis and are an easily accessible source for genealogists. All you need to know is the name and approximate year of death of your ancestor. The Calendar will provide you with:

> the address and occupation of the testator/testatrix
> the date of death
> the date of probate
> the person to whom the probate was granted
> an estimate of the total value of the goods and
>   the property of the deceased.

Thus, with very few initial details, it may be possible to locate a will and, in doing so, uncover a great deal of genealogical information.

The task is made even easier thanks to a consolidated index of testators, available in the main Record Office in Dublin. This has been prepared by the staff of the National Archives and covers the period 1858-77. The Ulster Historical Foundation has compiled a similar index for the period 1878-1900. These indexes are arranged according to the year of probate but, as already stated, probate may have taken place a few years after death, so therefore ensure that your search covers a period of up to ten years after death.

The Genealogical Office in Dublin has approximately 7,500 copies of destroyed wills that are scattered throughout various collections. Fortunately, an index to these wills has been compiled by P.B. Eustace and this has been published by the Irish Manuscripts Commission in its journal *Analecta Hibernica* No. 17. The Registry of Deeds in Dublin contains about 2,000 wills that are also scattered throughout various collections. An index of this collection has been published in *The Registry of Deeds: Abstracts of Wills* (1708-1785).

There are also collections of wills in:

> the Library of Trinity College, Dublin
> the National Library, Dublin
> the Royal Irish Academy, Dublin
> the Representative Church Body, Dublin.

In addition to this, there are many wills in solicitor records and in private papers throughout the country. Despite the obvious value of wills as a genealogical source for the period before 1858, they can be very difficult to locate but are an extremely rewarding source if unearthed.

Information Sources:
The 18th Century and Earlier

The Registry of Deeds

Since its foundation in 1708, the Registry of Deeds has been a major source of genealogical information. It is, perhaps, the single most important source for family historical information relating to the 18th century but because it is difficult to use, it is one of the most under-exploited genealogical sources.

The Registry of Deeds was established to facilitate land transactions in Ireland. During this period very few people owned land, but generally leased it from a landlord, middleman, the Established Church or the government. Although registration was voluntary in the early years, a surprisingly large number of people did use the Registry. Catholics and Presbyterians, however, tend to be under-represented.

The records in the Registry of Deeds fall into two main categories:
indexes
memorial books or deeds.

Memorial is the name given to the actual document and this can be located in the indexes either by location (townland) or by name of landlord. There are two separate indexes to the memorials – the Place Names Index and the Grantor's Index. You need to know the name of your ancestor's landlord or the townland address in order to use these records. For the 19th century, the name of the landlord can be obtained from Griffith's *Valuation* under the column headed 'immediate lessor'. Searchers should be aware that the names in the two indexes are not listed alphabetically but grouped under the initial letter; for example, all 'As' are grouped together, all 'Bs' grouped together, and so on. Remember, also, that registration may have taken place some time after the transaction was completed.

The main records in the Registry of Deeds are:
 contracts relating to leases
 mortgages
 land transfers
 marriage settlements
 deeds of trust
 business agreements
 wills.

To a first-time user, the memorials may appear intimidating, particularly because they are frequently couched in legal jargon. With perseverance, however, you can obtain a wealth of information. In detailing the transfer of land from one generation to another, wills and leases can name up to three generations of a family. Ages, addresses, family relationships and economic and social status can frequently be obtained from these documents.

The destruction of many original wills in the Public Record Office in 1922 has made the will collection in the Registry of Deeds more significant than it otherwise would have been. Approximately 2,000 survive for the period 1708-1800 alone. This collection of wills, abstracted and listed by P.B. Eustace, was first published in 1954 by the Irish Manuscripts Commission. The original indexes and memorials are located in The Property Registration Authority, Chancery St, Dublin 7. The Public Record Office of Northern Ireland also has a complete copy of these records.

Estate Records
Many landlords, especially the wealthier ones, kept estate records that detailed the various property transactions between them and their tenants. These records frequently included information on people who were casually employed on the estate or who were connected with it in some way, such as local tradesmen.

Collections of estate papers include:
> copies of leases
> maps
> wage books
> rent rolls
> correspondence between the landlord and his
> > agents (especially important in the case of
> > absentee landlords).

The most useful information is generally to be found in the leases and rent rolls, particularly if they name the sons and heirs of the tenant. A map will allow you to pinpoint the precise location of your ancestor's holding. Estate papers are not an easy source to use – some collections may contain thousands of documents and yet may not be indexed. Moreover, estate records do not survive for all parts of Ireland and some are still in private custody.

In order to use these records, you need to know the name of the estate on which your ancestor lived or worked. If you are unsure of the name of the local landlord, it can be obtained from Griffith's *Valuation*, under the column headed 'immediate lessor'.

The largest collections of estate records are held by the National Library of Ireland and the Public Record Office of Northern Ireland. A smaller collection is held by the National Archives in Dublin. A great many are still in private hands.

Flax Growers' Bounty List, 1796

Linen was Ireland's most important manufacturing industry during the 18th- and 19th centuries, although most of its manufacture was concentrated in Ulster. In 1711, a Linen Board was established to facilitate the expansion of the linen industry. To this end, the Board used a variety of means to encourage an expansion in the growth of flax in Ireland. In 1796, the Irish Linen Board published a list of 55,000 individuals who had received an award of a spinning-wheel or loom in return for planting flax. Those people who planted one acre were awarded four spinning-wheels, while a loom was given to those growing five acres. The county with the highest number of awards was Donegal, with over 7,000 spinning-wheels being awarded. County Tyrone was second. No list of awards exists for either County Dublin or County Wicklow.

This Bounty List is arranged by civil parish only and townland locations are not given. It provides the names of these 55,000 small farmers in Ireland, some thirty years before the Tithe Applotment Books start. This source is particularly useful because it will allow you to pinpoint the parish address of your ancestors at the end of the 18th century. The list is held by the Linenhall Library in Belfast, although the Public Record Office in Belfast has a microfiche copy of it, together with a very useful surname index arranged by county. The National Library in Dublin also has a copy.

Survey of Downpatrick, 1708

In 1708, James Maguire carried out a survey of the town of Downpatrick in County Down. The survey provides details of local property, the names of the tenants and the amount of rent paid. It has been published in *The City of Downe* by R.E. Parkinson, 1928. Although republished in 1977, this book is no longer in print but may be available from specialist libraries.

Protestant Householders, 1740

This is simply a list of Protestant householders in the Ulster counties of Antrim, Armagh, Londonderry, Donegal and Tyrone. It provides no further information apart from the householders' names. Although this list has not been printed, a typed, indexed copy is available for consultation in the Genealogical Office in Dublin.

'Census' of 1745

This early census covers parts of counties Galway, Roscommon and Sligo. Apart from giving information on the head of the household (occupation and religion), there are also details on children and servants. Occasionally the wife of the householder is mentioned by name. The fullness of the information provided in this census bears some resemblance to that collected in the 19th century, which makes it a very useful source. The census exists in manuscript form and is held by the National Archives in Dublin.

Militia Rolls and Pay Lists

At various times in the 17th- and 18th centuries the government required that local militia be maintained for the purpose of protection – either of the Protestant settlers or against invasion. The first Irish militia, which was exclusively Protestant, was raised in 1666 at the outbreak of war with France, the traditional Catholic enemy of England. In 1716, all Protestant males aged between 16 and 60 were required to 'muster' for four days each year. In 1756, the threat of invasion was felt to be real and, as a matter of urgency, all able-bodied male Protestants were required to take the usual oaths of Allegiance to the Crown. Various copies of these lists survive and are held by the National Archives in Dublin and the Public Record Office of Northern Ireland.

Religious Census, 1766

This census was commissioned by the government for the purpose of assessing the religious persuasion of the Irish population. Church of Ireland rectors were asked to compile returns of householders showing their religion – that is, whether Protestant, Dissenter or Papist (the common term for a Roman Catholic). Some rectors gave precise information, including names and addresses, whilst others merely provided totals. Unfortunately, all of the originals of this valuable record were destroyed in 1922. The copies that survive are scattered in various depositories, including the National Archives, the Representative Church Body and the Public Record Office of Northern Ireland.

Census of Carrick-on-Suir, 1799
This unique and valuable census provides detailed information relating to the names, addresses, ages, religion and occupations of almost 11,000 inhabitants of Carrick-on-Suir in County Tipperary in 1799. Although the original census is held in London, the National Library of Ireland holds a microfilm copy of it.

Voters' Lists, Poll Books and Freeholders' Records
These records were compiled for the purpose of listing people who were entitled to vote at elections. The Poll Books actually record the way in which people voted at these elections – secret ballots were adopted only in the late 19th century. These records can be useful because they provide the name and address of people entitled to vote and occasionally include personal details such as 'emigrated to America'.

Because universal suffrage (for men over 21 years of age and for women over the age of 30) was not introduced until 1918 (and it was 1928 before women over 21 could vote), the early records obviously relate only to a relatively small portion of the population and exclude women totally. Also, as a consequence of the repressive Penal Laws, Catholics were not entitled to vote in elections until 1793. Consequently, between 1727 and 1793, only Protestants with a freehold (land or tenement) valued at 40s per year had a vote. From 1793 to 1829, both Protestants and Catholics with freeholds valued at 40s could vote. However, in 1829, following Catholic Emancipation (when Catholics won the right to become Members of Parliament), people with freeholds valued at 40s lost their vote. Despite these restrictions, the records are useful in providing an address for an ancestor and a clear idea of his economic status.

Seventeenth-Century Records

During the 17th century, much land was confiscated by the government and subsequently redistributed to new owners. In order to keep track of these changes, the government ordered several surveys to be carried out. These surveys are not comprehensive but they are useful in providing a location for an ancestor in the 17th century. They also show who acquired and who lost land during this turbulent period. It is not surprising, therefore, that the government also required lists to be kept of people who were loyal and could be relied upon to carry arms if necessary.

Fortunately, many of these 17th-century lists have been printed. The main value of these records is that they provide a precise address for an ancestor in the 17th century, a period of great upheaval in Ireland. The following are the principal records for the 17th century.

Muster Rolls, 1631

Following the plantation of Ulster during the reign of James I of England, the larger landlords in Ireland were periodically required to muster their Protestant tenants for government inspection. These 'muster lists' or 'rolls' include the name, together with details of arms held by each person. Sometimes their places of origin in England or Scotland are also provided. Although age is rarely given, it can be assumed that these men were aged between 16 and 60 and were 'fit to bear arms'. Some of these records were destroyed in 1922. The surviving records are now available in the National Archives in Dublin and the Public Record Office of Northern Ireland. Records for a number of counties have been printed.

The Civil Survey, 1654-56

This survey was carried out under the provisions of the Act for the Satisfaction of Adventurers and Soldiers 1653, passed as part of the Cromwellian (Oliver Cromwell) confiscation of land in Ireland. Its purpose was to facilitate the transfer of forfeited estates owned by Irish landowners to 'adventurers', members of the army and the government who had supported Cromwell. It also enquired into land already owned by Protestant and English settlers and therefore was more comprehensive than the Down Survey. The Civil Survey was carried out by barony and was further subdivided into parishes and townlands. The name and religion of every proprietor in 1640, the extent of his land and its value was given. Catholics were referred to as 'Papists'. Although the original returns have been destroyed, copies for ten counties survive. These are held in the National Archives in Dublin and the Public Record Office in Northern Ireland. The Civil Survey has also been published.

Down Survey, 1654-59

This was intended to be a survey of all lands forfeited as a consequence of the Confederate War (1641-53). It affected about half of all lands in Ireland. It was carried out by an English physician, Sir William Petty, who agreed to complete it within one year and one month 'provided the weather was agreeable and the Tories (Irish outlaws) quiet'. In fact, it was not completed until 1659. In return, Petty received a reward of lands in Ireland, chiefly in County Kerry. The survey provides a mapped record of land ownership in Ireland, although its findings were also presented in tabulated form. It includes details of proprietors and their religion, as well as the value and average size of land held. Unfortunately, Protestants were not always included and so this survey is not complete. Most of the Down Survey was destroyed by fire in 1711, and the records that survived were subsequently destroyed in 1922. However, some copies still exist. This information has been printed and is readily available.

Petty also produced *Hiberniae Delineatio* in 1685, based on the Down Survey, which is regarded as the first general atlas of Ireland. Between 1682 and 1687, he wrote ten essays relating to the population of various cities, including Dublin.

Books of Survey and Distribution, *c.* **1661-81**
These volumes show the ownership of land in Ireland between 1661 and 1681, thus covering the Cromwellian and Restoration period. Some of the information is based on the Down Survey, so these books serve as a replacement for the destroyed originals. Copies of the books are available in the National Archives, Dublin and the Public Record Office in Northern Ireland. Unfortunately, the books for County Meath are not available.

Census of 1659
This census provides basic information regarding:
    the names of landlords (referred to as *tituladoes*)
    the number of tenants on their property
    whether they were English, Scottish or Irish.

The census does not survive for all of Ireland. Counties Cavan, Galway, Mayo, Wicklow and Tyrone are not included. The original is held at the Royal Irish Academy in Dublin, and the surviving returns have been published by the Irish Manuscripts Commission, Dublin.

Poll Tax Rolls, 1660
The purpose of this tax was to raise revenue for the government, and so people over a certain age were assessed according to their means. Many of these returns were destroyed in 1922.

Hearth Money Rolls, 1662-66
These Rolls relate to legislation of 1662 and subsequent years which required that a tax of 2 shillings should be levied on each hearth or fireplace. The purpose of this tax was to raise revenue for the government. The Hearth Money Rolls, therefore, provide a list of householders, the number of hearths for which they were taxed, and their address, by county, parish and townland. Although none of the original returns survive, copies exist for some counties. These have

been published by the Irish Manuscripts Commission in its journal, *Analecta Hibernica*, No. 24.

Subsidy Rolls, 1662-69
The purpose of these Rolls was to allow a tax to be levied on lands and possessions and paid to the Crown. Not all of these records have survived.

Miscellaneous Information Sources

Photographs

Photographs are sometimes overlooked as a source of evidence for family historians, yet, apart from providing valuable information, photographs have the unique advantage of instantly making your ancestors become more real and allowing them to assume their individual identity. Few people are lucky enough to inherit a fully referenced photograph album. It is more likely that during the course of your research you will amass a miscellaneous collection of photographs that will not include names, dates or locations.

Photography did not become widespread until the late 19th century. In the early years, most photographs would have been taken by professionals, of mainly wealthy and important subjects. As photography became less expensive, thousands of ordinary people had their likenesses taken at home, on holiday or in a studio. At the start of the 20th century, introduction of the Brownie, a relatively cheap camera, made amateur photography possible: the numbers of family photographs greatly increased.

The most useful photographs are those that include family groupings, such as wedding or christening photographs. Apart from the people who are present at such gatherings, note who was absent and try to find out why they were not there. Perhaps they were at war, ill or even dead. Bear in mind that group photographs include other people who were not necessarily members of the family, such as friends, work associates or neighbours. These people will help you to place your ancestors in a broader social context.

A photograph is most useful when it identifies the people in it and provides the date, location and occasion. Unfortunately, this is rarely the case and you may have to extract this information from clues within the photographs. For instance, it is always worth showing such photographs to other members of your family, particularly elderly ones. This might even jolt their memory and encourage them to reveal further useful reminiscences concerning your family.

Because most early photographs were studio portraits, the name and address of the studio, and perhaps a negative number, might be included on the photograph. This could help you identify the area in which your ancestors lived, and further information about the locality could then be found in a contemporary street directory. If the photograph studio still exists, it may have copies of old records and these will probably include the name and address of the person who commissioned the photograph, together with its cost, etc.

Occasionally, a costume can help you to date a photograph, although this can be misleading and you might need to seek an expert opinion. The majority of people would, for example, have had a 'Sunday best' outfit that was kept for special occasions and might already be ten years old when the photograph was taken.

Photographs can also be helpful in identifying the trade or profession of an ancestor. Further information can then be obtained in a local trade directory. Photographs of ancestors in military uniform are particularly useful, especially if you are able to identify the regiment in which your ancestor served. The background of a photograph can provide additional valuable information. A church, business premises, school or holiday resort, frequented by the family, can direct you to other collections of records. Photographs, apart from providing information on individual ancestors, will provide you with a social, economic and historical context in which to place them.

While photographs of people are probably of most interest, photographs of locations can help to put your ancestors in a geographical context. The largest collection of town photographs is the Lawrence Collection that covers the period 1870-1910 and consists of approximately 40,000 images. It is held in the National Library in Dublin, although some larger libraries may have a microfilm copy of it. It is indexed alphabetically, in order of place, and copies of negatives can be made. Smaller collections of photographic negatives held by the National Library include:

the Eason Collection, which consists of approximately
4,000 negatives covering the period 1910-30
the Valentine Collection which consists of approximately
3,000 negatives for the period 1930-50.

The Public Record Office of Northern Ireland has prints of some of the Lawrence collection as well as holding a number of other photographic collections including the Cooper archive, comprising approximately 2,500 photographs.

Workhouse Records

The Poor Law system was introduced to Ireland in 1838 and continued in the Republic of Ireland until 1923. It was not until l948 that it was finally abolished in Northern Ireland. It was in existence, therefore, during a period of crucial importance to family historians.

Poor Law Unions were important administrative units in 19th-century Ireland. Initially, Ireland was divided into 130 Poor Law Unions but this was increased to 163 during the Great Famine of 1845-52. Each Union contained a workhouse that took its name from the nearest market town, and it was into these institutions that poor and destitute people went to receive relief. Workhouses were governed by a Board of Guardians, usually local landowners or successful businessmen. It was not until the beginning of the 20th century that women were allowed to become Guardians.

Various categories of workhouse records have survived. The principal categories are:
the Minute Books of the Poor Law Guardians
the Admission Registers.

The Minute Books are most useful if your ancestor was a member of the Local Board of Guardians. Although they were not paid for performing this duty, there was considerable prestige in being able to write 'Poor Law Guardian' (PLG) after a surname. Each workhouse employed a large number of staff, ranging from masters and matrons to porters, schoolmasters and medical officers. If your ancestor worked in a workhouse, the Minute Books will usually provide details of his or her wages, job performance, etc.

If you suspect that your ancestor was ever in receipt of Poor Law relief, then the Admission Registers of the local workhouses are worth consulting. Unfortunately, not all these registers have survived, but where they do exist, a great deal of information about individuals can be obtained. This includes for each person:

> name
> age (or approximate if unknown)
> former address
> religion
> occupation
> date of admission
> date of departure.

Also, because people could only be admitted to a workhouse as part of a family unit, the admission registers will provide information on the whole family. Each workhouse also contained its own hospital and consequently housed a large number of sick and infirm people. The workhouse registers provide excellent information on each pauper's physical condition, including descriptions such as 'one leg', 'healthy', 'lousy', or 'very dirty'. In some unions, registers survive that list the births and deaths that took place within the workhouse. The numbers of people who died while inmates of the workhouse may seem high, but again this is largely due to the presence of the infirmary which often served the whole community.

The main value of workhouse records lies in the fact that they provide details about two, often forgotten, sections of society – the poor and the sick. Ancestors who were poor, illiterate and unemployed can be the most difficult to find. Workhouse records may, therefore, provide a vital clue to their whereabouts.

There are problems in using workhouse records, namely that they are bulky, rarely indexed, and scattered in various depositories throughout Ireland. The workhouse records of County Mayo, for example, are in the National Library in Dublin, while those for the South Dublin Union are held in the National Archives. The records for the other counties are generally held locally, usually in the county library. In Northern Ireland, these records have been centralised and the workhouse registers for counties Antrim, Armagh, Down, Fermanagh, Londonderry and Tyrone have been deposited in the Public Record Office in Belfast. For some Unions, extensive workhouse records have survived, but this is not always the case.

Many other 19th-century records were also arranged according to Poor Law Unions. The name of the local Union is provided as part of the address in the early civil records of births, deaths and marriages. For example, if you already know the townland or parish address of an ancestor and want to find out in which Poor Law Union it was situated, consult the *Townland Index of Ireland*.

Business Records

Business records often contain a great deal of detailed information relating to products, suppliers, customers and, most importantly, company employees. If you know that your ancestor was employed by a particular company that is still operative, check to see if their old records have survived. If the business has ceased to exist, company records may now be held by either the National Archives in Dublin or the Public Record Office of Northern Ireland. Since 1970, the Irish Manuscripts Commission has systematically surveyed the records of private businesses throughout the Republic and some of these are now deposited in the National Archives. The Public Record Office in Belfast also has a large collection of company records that are arranged in their Subject Index, according to trade or industrial process.

Generally, the most useful information relating to employees is to be found in the wages books, which occasionally include the age and address of the worker. Information relating to the owners, directors or trustees of a company will generally be found in the Minute Books or annual reports of the company.

British Army Records

A surprisingly large number of Irishmen served with the British Army in the 19th century. It has been estimated, for example, that in 1830 almost forty per cent of the British Army was Irish-born. Inevitably, these soldiers were stationed in many different places within the British Empire. Sometimes they obtained land and settled in the area in which they had served. This makes it difficult to establish where this ancestor was married or where he baptised his children.

The existence of extensive British Army records means that it is possible to obtain very full information on an army ancestor. In order to do this, you need to have some precise information on the person in question, such as the ancestor's army service number, or the name of the regiment in which he served, or the location of the regiment on a given date. If you do not already know these details, family memorabilia such as old medals, photographs, letters, etc. might provide the necessary information.

Records relating to colonial pensions in the 19th century have survived. So, if you do locate your ancestor in army records, you will discover a great deal of information about him. This includes:

his trade before enlisting

his father's occupation

his age

a full physical description of him, including height, colour of eyes and complexion

his military history, including length of service and conduct

details of any medals obtained

date and reasons for discharge.

These records may, therefore, provide the most complete description of your ancestor that you are ever likely to find.

A number of useful army records date back to the early 18th century. In 1679, King Charles II established the Royal Hospital in Kilmainham in Dublin (the Royal Hospital in Chelsea was not set up until 1681). At this stage, Ireland and England maintained separate army establishments which were joined by the Act of Union of 1800. Pension records survive from 1702. Irish soldiers who left the army with a disabling injury or as invalids were entitled to a pension from Kilmainham, and this practice continued until 1822. Pension books are arranged by date of medical examination, so it is necessary to know the approximate date of the granting of the pension.

All British Army records are held in The National Archives, Ruskin Avenue, Kew, Richmond, Surrey, TW9 4DU, England. If you are unable to visit Kew, it is possible to commission a searcher to undertake a search of the records on your behalf.

Royal Irish Constabulary Records
The records of the Royal Irish Constabulary are a rarely used source. However, if your ancestor served with this body, it can offer a fascinating insight into his life. Records start in 1816, when a Peace Preservation Force was established in Ireland. This was later extended into County Constabulary Forces in 1822, and in 1836 it became the Irish Constabulary. The Royal prefix was granted later in the century. Dublin continued to maintain its own police force, known as the Dublin Metropolitan Police, established in 1786.

In 1922, the records of the Constabulary were taken to England and they are now deposited in the National Archive in Kew. The National Archives in Dublin and the Public Record Office in Northern Ireland, however, have microfiche copies of these records.

These records contain many useful personal details including:

> date of joining the force
> age at joining
> previous trade
> marital status
> native county of wife (but usually not her name)
> place of birth
> name of the person who recommended the recruit.

Because members of the Constabulary would have served in different parts of the country, the records also list:

> the locations in which he was stationed
> details of any promotion
> length of service
> date of retirement and/or death.

A fascinating detail included is the height of each member of the Constabulary!

The wealth of information available in these records will enable you to search for details of your ancestor's birth, his marriage and any children he may have had. It will also enable you to follow his movements throughout the country.

Protest Petitions

These are an unusual and rewarding source for any family historian to use.

Anti-Repeal Petition

The Public Record Office in Northern Ireland holds an 1848 Anti-Repeal Petition for County Down as part of the Downshire Papers. This document is arranged by parish and contains approximately 10,000 names, including the occupations of the signatories. Repealers were people who wanted a repeal of the Act of Union of 1800. They wanted Ireland to have an independent parliament. The Anti-Repeal Movement consisted of those who wanted to maintain the links with Great Britain forged by the Act of Union.

Police Reports on the Fenians

The National Archives in Dublin has a large collection of police reports describing Fenian suspects in the 1860s (they were formerly housed in the State Paper Office in Dublin Castle). Fenians were nationalists who wished to end the political union with Great Britain. These reports are fully indexed.

Home Rule Petitions (The Covenant)

At the beginning of the 20th century there was a crisis in Ireland caused by the prospect of Home Rule. This was particularly intense in the north-eastern part of Ulster where the majority of the population were Presbyterians. The Unionists, as they were known, wished to maintain the historic link with Britain established by the Act of Union of 1800. They were apprehensive that a Home Rule Act was about to be passed that would give Ireland her own independent parliament, based in Dublin. Various protest activities were organised. One of the most spectacular took place in Belfast in September 1912, when a day of action was arranged, culminating in the signing of the Solemn League and Covenant. Over a quarter of a million men signed this Covenant, with a supporting Declaration signed by almost as many women. The signatories usually provided their precise address, and this is useful in helping to locate them in the 1911 census. The signed copies of the Covenant are now held by the Public Record Office of Northern Ireland. It is also available as a searchable online database on the PRONI website.

School Registers

Old school registers are an under-exploited yet extremely useful source of information. They contain a wealth of information and can be regarded as another form of census substitute. Although private, church and 'hedge' schools existed in Ireland in the early part of the 19th century, a State-run system of education was not created until 1831, when the Board of Commissioners for National Education established a system of primary schools. The following are the records of this body and cover the period 1831-1921:

National School Applications: these list schools that made applications to enter the national system of education, or who required grant aid from the Board. These records contain detailed information about the school premises, the names of the teachers, the subjects taught, the number of pupils and the average daily attendance.

Salary Books: these provide details of the salaries paid to every teacher who had been recognised by the National Board. (Both National School Applications and Salary Books are particularly valuable if an ancestor was a teacher.)

School Registers: these contain detailed information on each pupil. This includes either the date of birth or the age when he or she started school, religion, the occupation and address of father, the name of the school previously attended and details of attendance and academic progress. A column reserved for general observations includes such insights as 'left school to work on farm' or 'emigrated', or even 'died'.

In addition to the fascinating information which they contain, school registers are useful for providing a valuable link with other records. The age of each pupil, for example, gives a date that will enable you to search for a record of birth. The early schools were non-denominational, so the inclusion of religious persuasion is useful. Roman Catholics were listed as 'RC', Presbyterians as 'P' and members of the Established Church as 'EC'. The occupation of the father can also be useful. If he was no longer alive, the register often notes that the mother is a widow. The school previously attended can be very useful for tracing where the family originated, especially if they moved from the country to a large city. There is an alphabetical index at the front of each book. A quick glance at this will establish whether your ancestor attended a particular school and if he or she had siblings.

In the Republic of Ireland these records are scattered in various locations. The majority are held by the National Archives, whilst a number are still held locally, either in schools or in churches. The National Archives also has the largest collection of salary books, school applications, registers and files relating to the period before 1922. In Northern Ireland, the largest collection of school records is held by the Public Record Office, which has approximately 1,500 registers for the 19th century.

Directories
Street and trade directories are a useful source for family historians as they frequently provide information that may not be readily available elsewhere. They often include useful background information on individual towns or counties in Ireland. They can also provide information of a more specialised nature, such as the names of all people involved in the medical profession or lists of judges, etc.

Their most practical use, however, is in providing precise addresses for people who lived in the larger towns, as well as for those who belonged to any identifiable group or profession, such as 'gentry and nobleman', 'pawnbrokers', 'grocers' or 'wine merchants'. Although a number of directories date back to the 18th century, they tend to be comparatively rare and do not contain as much detailed information as the later ones.

Here is a list of useful directories (presented alphabetically by author):

Bassett, George Henry, *The Book of County Tipperary* first published in 1880. This book is part of a series that includes other counties and is being reprinted by Friar's Bush Press, Belfast

Bradshaw, Thomas, *General Directory of Newry, Armagh, Dungannon, Portadown, Tandragee, Lurgan, Waringstown, Banbridge, Warrenpoint, Rostrevor, Kilkeel and Rathfriland* (1819)
The Catholic Directory, Almanack and Registry (1836)

Griffith, George, *County Wexford Almanac* (1872)

Lee, Samuel Percy, *Ecclesiastical Register: Church of Ireland* (1814)

Lucas, Richard, *Cork Directory* (1787)

Martin, Matthew, *Belfast Directory* (1841)

McComb, William, *Presbyterian Almanack* (1857)
Pigot, J., *City of Dublin and Hibernian Provincial Directory* (1820, 1824, 1846, 1856, 1870, 1881, 1894)
Slater, J., *National Commercial Directory of Ireland* (published intermittently from 1846-1894)
Thom, A., *Almanac and Official Directory* (published annually from 1844)
Watson, John, *Dublin Directory* (1729 onwards).

Directories are an excellent source, especially for ancestors who resided in the towns. However, they appeared irregularly, and were often out of date by the time they were published, so locating an ancestor in them can often be a question of luck. Also, as they are a scattered source, it may not be easy to locate the particular directory required. The largest collections of directories can be found in the National Library of Ireland, Trinity College, Dublin, and the Linenhall Library, Belfast. Smaller collections are held by the National Archives, Dublin, and the Public Record Office of Northern Ireland. The most comprehensive list of directories has been compiled by R. Ffolliett and D. Begley, and is published in *Irish Genealogy: A Record Finder*, edited by D. Begley (1981).

Ordnance Survey Memoirs

The *Ordnance Survey Memoirs* are the written records of the staff of the Ordnance Survey (army officers) made while carrying out fieldwork for the compilation of Ordnance Survey maps of Ireland in the 1820s and 1830s. Initially, when the Board of Ordnance was established in 1791, the research was carried out in anticipation of an invasion by France. By the 1820s, this fear had passed and the survey was regarded as a way of smoothing out inequities in the local taxation system. This level of survey necessitated the drawing up of a map which was, uniquely at the time, six inches to one mile. Because this level of detail included even townlands, the map is officially referred to as *The Townland Survey of Ireland*. The field books were kept to ensure that the survey was thorough and accurate.

It is unfortunate that these books are often neglected as a genealogical source as they provide useful background information on various localities. They describe in detail the 'natural features, the ancient and modern topography, and the present state of the people' in the parishes visited by the officers. For family historians, the information about the local inhabitants of each area visited is particularly useful, and some of the *Memoirs* include lists of people who emigrated from the area in the 1830s.

Sadly, these *Memoirs* only cover the northern parts of the country and, even then, they are not complete. Each *Memoir* varies greatly in the degree of detail provided: the *Memoir* for Enniskillen (171 pages long), for example, is regarded as an excellent one. The following extract from the *Memoir* for Ballymena will give some indication of the richness (and bluntness) of this source:

> 'The Ballymena people are neither politic nor aristocratic in their manners, nor do they possess any taste. The gentlemen in business, though they are wealthy and live comfortably, seem to think that any intercourse with strangers would tend to disturb their domestic arrangements and interfere with their privacy and they, therefore, take no notice of them. They are rather a moral race, though the number of public houses, there being 107, would lead one to suppose otherwise.'

The original manuscripts of the *Ordnance Survey Memoirs* are located in the Royal Irish Academy, Dublin. Both the National Library and the Public Record Office in Northern Ireland have microfilm copies.

The surviving *Memoirs* for all parishes have been published by the Institute of Irish Studies, Belfast, in association with the Royal Irish Academy. In total, forty volumes of *Ordnance Survey Memoirs* were published between 1990 and 1998. Excellent background information on this source is also available in J.H. Andrews' *History in the Ordnance Map: An Introduction for Irish Readers* (1993).

Maps

If you know the place of origin or the address where your ancestor lived, a map will help you to pinpoint this location precisely. Apart from telling you about the actual physical terrain of your ancestor's locality, a map can also be useful in helping you to answer questions such as:

> what church did he or she worship in?
> which school did he or she attend?
> in which graveyard was he or she buried?

During the 19th century, when most travelling would have been done on foot, the answer to all of these questions is, probably, 'the nearest one'.

Although maps are available for different periods of Irish history, they vary greatly in terms of accuracy and amount of detail. The art of *cartography* (map drawing) only really became widespread in the 17th century. This was partly to enable the government to chart the process of new land settlements that were taking place – in particular, the plantation of Ulster at the beginning of the century. Most of the maps from this period are concerned with military activity and territorial distribution. It is not surprising, therefore, that forts and fortifications are prominent features.

In the 19th century the government decided that, in order to value property accurately for the purposes of collecting taxes, detailed maps of the whole country were needed. In 1791, the Ordnance Survey was established, which was responsible for centralising and standardising the maps of Ireland. By 1846 it had compiled almost 2,000 sheets on the scale of six inches to one statute mile (with towns on an even larger scale) and covered the whole of the country. These maps were used by Richard Griffith in his *Valuation*. By using the map reference number in the left-hand column of the *Valuation*, it is possible to locate precisely where your ancestor held his or her property.

The most extensive map collections relating to the 19th century are held by the National Library, Dublin and the Public Record Office of Northern Ireland. Copies of some 19th-century maps can be purchased from the Ordnance Survey Office, Phoenix Park, Dublin.

Earlier maps that may be useful include:
    the Down Survey maps (1654-59), available
      in various scales and cover all counties except
      Galway and Roscommon
    Roque's map of Dublin for 1756
    The Trinity College, Dublin, Maps, with the names of
      the families holding possessions in each district.

Newspapers

Newspapers were published in Ireland from the late 17th century onwards but it was not until the 18th century that they became widespread. By the 19th century they had proliferated to such an extent that virtually every provincial town in Ireland had at least one newspaper. A surprisingly large number of these papers have survived. Ireland can also boast the oldest surviving newspaper in Europe, the *Belfast Newsletter*, the first edition of which was published in 1737.

The newspapers of the 17th- and 18th centuries contain relatively little information of genealogical value. The most useful articles are those relating to marriages and deaths, although only the middle and upper classes would have used this medium for such announcements. Notices of birth are quite rare due to the high level of infant mortality and, where they do exist, they rarely mention either the mother or child by name. A typical entry might read: 'The wife of George Thompson, Esquire, this day delivered a daughter'. Again, it would only be those people of substantial means who would have used newspapers in this way. However, in the 18th century, before the compulsory registration of births, deaths and marriages, a notice in a newspaper might be the only record of such an event. Also, because of the non-denominational nature of many newspapers, they are a particularly good source when attempting to locate wealthy Catholic ancestors.

By the 19th century, newspapers were providing more information of genealogical interest. Notices of births, deaths and marriages were increasingly recorded, although the poorest sections of society would not have used them. Obituaries also became more common, and included people who died overseas. The fascination of 19th-century newspapers, however, is also attributable to the diverse and miscellaneous articles that they carried. These could include:

minutes of the local Boards of Guardians
lists of subscribers to relief funds
descriptions of 'freaks' who were touring the country
descriptions of people who attended society balls
names of the heroic dead who died on behalf of King
    and country in some far-flung part of the
    British Empire.

Newspapers from the 19th century are particularly useful if you had an ancestor who was a convict, as crime cases were reported with great relish. Consider, for example, the richness of the following extracts:

At Down Assizes, Sophia Branigan was found guilty of stealing wearing apparel at Belville, the property of William Henry. To be burned in the hand.'
Source: *Freeman's Journal*, 13 August 1799

At Dublin City Sessions, Maria Stratford was charged with taking from the person of Edward Riley, a silver watch. This incident originated in one of the ordinary accidents of 'en passant' nocturnal love. In deep shade, Maria, the immodest, used her charms to arrest the attention of the jovial cit.'
Source: *Freeman's Journal*, 27 September 1800

Cork City Assizes, Catherine Molloy, alias "Pretty Kitty" (from her remarkable ugliness), was arraigned for stealing £10 from Humphrey Thomas, a stout, well-looking country fellow, stating that he was a pig dealer. In cross examination, he said he was not drunk when the money was taken from him, for he was under a bond of conscience not to take more than a noggin of whiskey and four pints of port every day. Prisoner was found guilty and being an old well known inhabitant of the gaol was sentenced to seven years transportation.'

Source: *Freeman's Journal,* 17 April 1823

If you have a criminal ancestor, therefore, a report in a local newspaper could be the key to finding out more about his or her chequered past. If you discover that he or she was transported to Australia, the search will then take on a whole new dimension.

If you had an ancestor who was engaged in a trade or a profession, local newspapers can offer various insights into his or her activities. This can take the form of advertisements, notices of expansion, bankruptcy, address changes, transfer of ownership, etc. Newspapers sometimes included profiles of local successful businessmen or merchants, especially in obituaries.

In the 19th century particularly, a large amount of space was devoted to emigration: advertisements to attract emigrants; descriptions of overseas colonies; and letters from successful emigrants. Newspapers, therefore, reflect social and economic life in Ireland at any given time.

Newspapers, however, are not an easy source to use. Searching them can be time consuming if the precise date of an event is not known. It is therefore advisable to use any indexes that may exist. An index to biographical information found in the *Dublin Journal* (1763-1771), is held by the National Library of Ireland, and copies of the birth, death and marriage notices from the *Belfast Newsletter* (1737-1800), are held in the Linenhall Library, Belfast. The London *Times*, which carried many articles of Irish interest, has been indexed by Palmer, and copies are available in most libraries.

Newspapers are also difficult to use because they are a very scattered source. The largest collection of Irish newspapers is found in the British Library Newspapers, Colindale Avenue, London NW9 5HE. Within Ireland, the largest collections are held by the National Library, Dublin and the Linenhall Library, Belfast, although the Central Library in Belfast also has an excellent collection which is being continually extended. The Public Record Office of Northern Ireland, in conjunction with the Library Association (Northern Ireland branch), has published a useful booklet entitled *Northern Ireland Newspapers: Checklist with Locations*. Unfortunately there is no similar publication for the Republic of Ireland. While a lot of valuable genealogical information is found in newspapers even a determined effort may not uncover it.

Marriage Licence Bonds, 1629-1864

For most of the 17th- and 18th centuries, marriages between people of different denominations and those performed by Dissenting ministers were illegal in Ireland. Some Roman Catholics and Presbyterians, therefore, chose to be married in the Established Church. To enable this ceremony to be performed, they would either ask the minister to publish banns or purchase a licence from the bishop of the diocese.

Although banns were the cheapest and most widely used form of proclamation, only a small number of them have survived. If a couple desired to marry immediately, they would have to purchase a special licence to do so. Before the licence was granted, the couple had to enter a bond at a Diocesan Court. These bonds included details such as:

> the names of the bride and groom
> their ages and residences
> marital status (bachelor, widow, etc.)
> the intended place of marriage
> the names of their two sureties.

This information had to be guaranteed against a surety which could be as high as £500. Unfortunately, most of the bonds and licences were destroyed in 1922. However, the indexes to many of them, and some abstracts, have survived. These records are available in the National Archives in Dublin or the Public Record Office in Northern Ireland.

Parliamentary Papers
One of the principal sources for gaining an insight into local conditions during the period from 1800 to 1921 is British Parliamentary Papers. These papers often contain reports of committees and commissioners who were carrying out research on behalf of the government into the state of Ireland. They contain a great deal of material on topics such as education, literacy and poverty. For family historians, their value lies in the wealth of local data that they provide.

The International Genealogical Index (IGI)
As the name suggests, it is an international index (on microfiche) of genealogical information. The International Genealogical Index is mostly based on information taken from parish registers. There are currently over 118 million names on the International Index. The part of the index relating to Ireland can be used as a starting point in any search although, unless your surname is unusual, it might be difficult to prove that the entry refers to your ancestor. This index is updated every few years and is available in major repositories and branch libraries in Ireland. The headquarters of the Church of Jesus Christ of Latter-Day Saints is 50 East North Temple, Salt Lake City, Utah 84150.

Information Technology
Over the last few years, an increasing amount of genealogical information has become available in the form of CDs and DVDs or on the internet. These sources are increasing at a very rapid rate. Family tree programs are also useful as they provide an easy way of preserving and organising information. A number of family historians have also created

websites relating to the surnames that they are searching. These sources are well worth using although you can never be certain of the accuracy of the data. You could even create your own family name website.

A large number of Record Offices, libraries and family history organisations also have a website and this is a quick and effective way of finding out about their collections and there opening hours.

Useful Websites
More and more material is becoming available on-line. Some of the best sites for anyone trying to trace their family tree are:

www.ancestryireland.com
www.emeraldancestors.com
www.familysearch.com
www.findmypast.com
www.genesreunited.com
www.ifhf.brsgenealogy.com
www.irelandroots.com
www.irishoriginsnetwork.com
www.irish-roots.net
www.nationalarchives.gov.uk
www.nationalarchives.ie
www.proni.gov.uk
www.rascal.ac.uk

Software Packages
Software packages for family historians are readily available and increasingly more sophisticated. It is even common-place for new computers to include family history software. As changes in software occur so rapidly, it is difficult to keep pace with the changes, although most versions will offer a free upgrade.

Before purchasing a software package, check that it is compatible with your existing system. Also, look to see if it provides a tutorial, technical support and useful search tools.

Recommended software is the latest version of *Family Tree Maker for Windows* (www.familytreemaker.com) and *Legacy 7.0 Family Tree* (www.LegacyFamilyTree.com) also for use on Windows.

The Irish Overseas

Since the 18th century, emigration has been an important part of the life-cycle of Irish people. Between 1801 and 1921, at least eight million people emigrated from Ireland. Most people living in Ireland today will have at least one ancestor who took the emigrant ship in order to seek his or her fortune abroad.

During the 18th century, approximately 250,000 people left Ireland, mainly to settle in the United States of America. These people were predominantly Presbyterians from Ulster. They were descended from the Scots Presbyterians who had settled in Ulster in the previous century and they were referred to in North America as Ulster Scots or Scots Irish. Nineteenth-century emigrants, especially after the Famine, tended to come from all parts of Ireland, although a high percentage hailed from the poorest areas in the west of the country. They were also overwhelmingly Catholic.

In both centuries, however, once under way, emigration gained its own momentum. Letters home encouraged friends, neighbours and other members of the family to leave Ireland and, even more importantly, these letters often included the fare to America, either by pre-paid ticket or by supplying cash to purchase a ticket. For those who were young, healthy and single, the promise of a better life provided an irresistible incentive to take the emigrant boat. One unkind 19th century observer, Sir William Wilde (census commissioner and father of Oscar) went so far as to describe those who had been left behind in Ireland as 'the poor, the weak, the old, the lame, the sick, the blind, the dumb, the imbecile and insane'.

For the most part, the destination of the majority of 19th-century emigrants continued to be North America, although there was extensive Irish settlement in every English-speaking country in the world, and substantial numbers migrated to less familiar places such as Latin America. Apart from employment opportunities in North America, an added incentive to choose this destination was that the passage was relatively cheap – about £5 per adult – and the journey took only about six weeks. In contrast to this, the cost of travelling to Australia, for example, was about three times as expensive and the journey took about five months. It is not surprising, therefore, that emigrants to both Australia and New Zealand in the 19th century were State-assisted, their passage usually being paid for by the government.

Destination of Irish emigrants (per cent)

	1851	1871
Canada	9	8
United States	39	50
Australia	2	4
Britain	9	24

Irish emigrants were by no means a homogeneous group. They came from a wide variety of social and economic backgrounds and religious and political persuasions. Irish emigration differed from that of other countries in that at least fifty per cent of the migrants were women. Inevitably, the effect of large-scale emigration was to alter Irish society, while the influx of large numbers of Irish people to the host country irreversibly changed the course of its history. If your ancestor was an emigrant – whether a politician, convict, bush-ranger or, more probably, one of the anonymous masses – he or she would have played a part in shaping the history of two countries: the country of birth and the country of death.

Searching in your Home Country

If you are trying to trace an ancestor who took the emigrant ship in the 18th-, 19th- or even 20th century, the logical place to start the search for that person is in the country to which they emigrated. The initial steps are similar to those followed when pursuing an exclusively Irish ancestor:

1. Ask members of your family to share their recollections with you.
2. Try to locate old memorabilia, including family bibles, photographs, naturalisation papers, etc. Gravestone inscriptions or obituaries are particularly useful as they often state the exact place of birth.

3.   Find out background information on the original ancestor, for example, surname, place of birth and possible reasons for emigrating. This information can be located in a local reference library.

4.   Search the official and legal records, concentrating particularly on shipping records and emigration papers, where they exist.

During each of the above stages, it is important to try to establish the following information:

> where the original emigrant was from, preferably
>   the townland or the parish
> his or her religion in Ireland.
> his or her dates of birth, marriage and death
> when and by what means he or she emigrated.

If you find any relevant information, make sure that you write it down in full, including the source from which you obtained it and the reference number of the document that provided it.

There are, unfortunately, few surviving records of the vast number of people who emigrated as independent, paying passengers, although the records are generally better for the small minority who were government-assisted. For the most part, the onus was on the government of the host country to keep these records. You should not expect to find extensive emigration records in Ireland. Exceptions to this are:

passenger lists for the period 1803-6, compiled under the Passenger Act of 1803 and held in the British Library in London

details of emigrants in the *Ordnance Survey Memoirs* for counties Londonderry and Antrim in the 1830s: the originals are held in the Royal Irish Academy in Dublin but they have been published

the records of three business firms (J. and J. Cooke, Robert Taylor and Co. and McCorkell of Londonderry) who specialised in emigration to North America between the 1840s and 1870s.

Copies of the above are available in the two principal Record Offices in Ireland. Unfortunately, these records vary considerably in the type of information they provide and sometimes do not include a precise place of origin.

There are various other miscellaneous sources for a study of emigration. A sometimes overlooked source, for example, is the letters of the emigrants themselves, although they are inevitably scattered. Over the last few years, however, the Public Record Office in Northern Ireland has systematically built up such a collection, and it now includes several thousand documents. These have now, along with material from other archives and libraries, been compiled into a searchable database by the Centre for Migration Studies at the Ulster American Folk Park. This Emigration Database is available in selected libraries and Record Offices, including the Public Record Office of Northern Ireland.

Emigrants' letters are an excellent source because they refer to entire family networks. They usually also include both a date and an address and, consequently, they help to chart the movements of the emigrants themselves.

A useful, but by no means exhaustive, short-cut is provided by the Emigrant Index of the Surname Archive. This is a list of emigrants, circa 1600-1850, from England, Wales, Scotland and Ireland. If you are at an apparent dead end it may be worthwhile, for the small fee, to commission a search from this index. The address is 108 Sea Lane, Ferring, West Sussex, England. There is also an emigration centre in The Windmill, Blennerville, County Kerry, Ireland.

If you live overseas and decide to commission a professional genealogist to continue the Irish side of the search on your behalf, it is essential to provide the searcher with as much detailed information as possible. Alternatively, if you intend to visit Ireland yourself to continue your family research, it is essential that you undertake preparatory work in your home country.

Before visiting Ireland, you should check the website for FAQ (Frequently Asked Questions) or 'Visiting Us' information of the repositories you intend to visit. If need be, contact them directly in order to ascertain their opening hours and whether it is necessary to book in advance to use their facilities. It would be a pity to arrive in Ireland to find that their holiday arrangements coincide exactly with yours! Generally, the more background work you do in your home country, the higher the chances of success when the search moves to Ireland.

England and Wales
After 1169, under the leadership of Strongbow, a number of Anglo-Normans settled in Ireland, initially in Wexford and Waterford. Strongbow eventually became Lord of Leinster. Gradually, the Anglo-Normans extended their control into other parts of Ireland. The political link, established in the 12th century, proved to be enduring and was to shape the subsequent histories of both England and Ireland. However, for many native Irish, this connection was not a welcome one. In 1800, the Act of Union between Great Britain and Ireland again changed the political relationship between the two countries. Increasingly, the two economies became interdependent. In the 19th century particularly, the industrialising British economy provided an accessible labour market for many Irish people, with London, Liverpool and Glasgow the main areas of settlement. Surprisingly, a large number of Irish men chose to join the British Army. If your ancestor, therefore, 'took the King's shilling' (i.e. joined the armed forces) in one form or another, it may be worthwhile searching army records in Britain.

In general, the collection of information by the State started earlier in England and Wales than in Ireland. The State registration of births, deaths and marriages began in England and Wales in July 1837, when civil registration of those events was made compulsory by the government. In Ireland it did not start until 1864.

Census Returns

The first government census in England and Wales was taken in 1801, and every 10 years thereafter, although few of the early returns have survived. Moreover, these early returns contain little information of use to the family historian. Virtually all of the 1841 returns survive, although they are not as comprehensive as later ones. For example, marital status was not recorded in 1841, nor was relationship to the head of the household. The 1851 census, therefore, is regarded as the most useful early return. This census is valuable for Irish people who migrated to England because it asked people where they were born, and Irish people living in England usually wrote down 'I' or 'Ireland'. Occasionally, a specific townland or county is named.

Census records for England and Wales from 1841 to 1901 are available online at The National Archives website (www.nationalarchives.gov.uk). It is free to search the website, but there is a small charge to download images of individual census entries.

The Family Records Centre

The Family Records Centre, which used to be based in Myddleton St, London, has closed. However, a useful website: www.familyrecords.gov.uk, will point researchers in the right direction. Meanwhile, for births, marriages, deaths, adoptions and civil partnerships go to the General Register Office website: www.gro.gov.uk

Census returns, wills and other material formerly held by the Family Records Centre are now held by The National Archives, Ruskin Avenue, Kew: website: www.nationalarchives.gov.uk

The National Archive, Kew

This Record Office houses one of the largest historical archives in the world. It also holds records that are valuable to family historians. It has produced a number of excellent leaflets describing these records. Its early collections include:

Records of Chancery Proceedings, from the
14th century
Close Rolls, from the 16th to 19th centuries
Hearth Tax Returns for the 17th century
Death Duty Registers and Indexes from 1796 onwards
Unauthenticated Marriage Registers, which relate
to clandestine marriages in the London area in
the 17th- and 18th centuries
Apprenticeship Books and Indexes for 1710-1811
Land Tax Redemption Assessments, a register
of all owners of property who paid land tax in 1798.

A useful starting point for using this Record Office is the website: www.nationalarchives.gov.uk
The full address is The National Archives, Ruskin Avenue, Kew, Richmond, Surrey TW9 4DU (Telephone: +44 (0) 20 8876 3444).

Borthwick Institute of Historical Research

Before the introduction of central registration in England, wills were proved in a variety of churches and courts. The Borthwick Institute holds records of the Prerogative Court of York. The full address of the Borthwick Institute of Historical Research is University of York, Heslington, York, YO10 5DD (Telephone: +44 (0) 1904 32 1166). Will indexes from 1853-59 are available on-line under the auspices of British Origins: www.originsnetwork.com.

County Record Offices

These offices usually contain extensive collections of records that are valuable to the family historian, especially those relating to the local area. Some parish registers have been deposited in County Record Offices, but if you would like to visit the church in the parish where your ancestor resided, you will find the name and address of the present incumbent in *Crockford's Clerical Directory*. County Record Offices also house collections of wills. Most Record Offices now have their own dedicated websites and it is worth doing a search of Google to find them.

Other Useful Addresses
Federation of Family History Societies
PO Box 8857, Lutterworth, LE17 9BJ
Telephone: +44 (0) 1455 20 3133
Email: info@ffhs.org.uk
Website: www.ffhs.org.uk

British Library Newspapers, Colindale Avenue,
London, NW9 5HE
Telephone: +44 (0) 20 7412 7353
Email: newpaper@bl.uk
Website: www.bl.uk/onlinegallery/visits/colindale.html

Society of Friends, Friends' House,
173-177 Euston Road, London NW1 2BJ
Telephone: +44 (0) 20 7663 1000
Website: www.quaker.org.uk/library

Channel Islands Family History Society
CIFHS, PO Box 57, Jersey JE4 5TN
Telephone: +44 (0) 1481 72 1732
Website: www.channelislandshistory.com

Manx Museum and National Trust
Library and Art Gallery, Douglas, Isle of Man, IM1 3LY
Telephone: +44 (0) 1624 64 8000
Website: www.gov.im/mnh/heritage/museums/
    manxMuseum.xml

The National Library of Wales
Aberystwyth, Ceredigion, Wales, SY23 3BU
Telephone: +44 (0) 1970 63 2800
Website: www.llgc.org.uk

Scotland

Scotland and Ireland – particularly the north-eastern part of Ireland – have many historical links that existed long before the Plantation of Ulster in the 17th century. This is partly due to the geographical proximity of the two regions. Apart from the many Scottish Presbyterians who chose to settle in Ulster, many Ulster people travelled to Scotland in the hope of finding either seasonal or permanent employment. It is highly probable, therefore, that if your ancestors hailed from Ulster, you will have at least one Scottish forbear. Most records of genealogical value in Scotland are located in Edinburgh and the following are the two main depositories:

New Register House

The civil registration of births, deaths and marriages began in Scotland in 1855 – nine years before civil registration in Ireland. The information contained in these certificates varies according to the year. The 1855 certificates, for example, apart from the usual details, also provide information on:

> the place of birth of both the mother and father
> the year and place of marriage
> the number of living and deceased children.

In 1856, however, this was modified as it was considered too impractical to record so much information.

Information on births, deaths and marriages for the period before 1855 can be found in local parish registers. These are also held in New Register House. The earliest parish registers were started in the late 16th century although most began in the 17th century. Unfortunately, due to wars and periods of religious repression, not all parish registers survive. The amount of information they contain also varies greatly. New Register House has records from almost 1,000 parishes.

The first census return was taken in Scotland in 1841 and every 10 years subsequently. The censuses for 1841, 1851, 1861, 1871, 1881 and 1891 are available for public consultation at New Register House. These census returns vary slightly in the type of information they provide, the later ones usually providing more accurate and detailed information. In the 1841 census, for example, age is given to the nearest 5 or 0 (e.g. 46 is rounded to 45, while 42 is rounded to 40). In the 1851 census, however, age is given precisely (although people were notoriously inaccurate when giving their ages). Later censuses included questions such as: can you speak Gaelic? How many children go to school? and so on.

As you can see, many valuable Scottish genealogical records are conveniently housed under one roof. The public can visit New Register House though it is necessary to pay a fee before you search the records. New Register House also undertakes searches by post for a fee.

The full address of New Register House is:
Registrar General of Scotland, New Register House,
3 West Register St, Edinburgh EH1 3YT
Telephone: +44 (0) 131 334 0380
Website: www.gro-scotland.gov.uk

National Archives Scotland

Formerly the Scottish Record Office, this repository contains a large number of records of value. Wills, with few exceptions, are housed here. Scottish wills have survived from 1514 and are an excellent source of information. It is interesting to note that old Scottish law forbade people from leaving land or buildings in a will, only permitting them to leave movable property.

Sasines – peculiarly Scottish records – are also deposited in this office. They date from 1599 to 1868 and list the owners, but not the tenants, of land all over Scotland. In order to use them, you need to know the approximate date of residence and locality in which your ancestors resided. The sasine will, in turn, provide you with details of heirs, relationships and various property transactions.

The full address of the National Archives Scotland is:
National Archives Scotland, HM General Register House,
2 Princes St, Edinburgh EH1 3YY
Telephone: +44 (0) 131 535 1314
Website: www.nas.gov.uk

Other Useful Addresses
Scottish Genealogy Society
15 Victoria Terrace, Edinburgh EH1 2JL
Telephone: +44 (0) 131 220 3677
Website: www.scotsgenealogy.com

Scottish Ancestry Research Society
8 York Road, Edinburgh EH5 3EH
Telephone: +44 (0) 131 552 2028
Website: www.scotsancestry.co.uk

United States of America
The United States has long been a favoured destination for Irish emigrants. In the 18th century, approximately a quarter of a million people, mainly Presbyterians from Ulster, emigrated to colonial America. This high level of emigration continued into the 19th century, largely as a result of the Great Famine of 1845-52. It is estimated that of the two million people who left Ireland between 1846 and 1855, the vast majority went to North America. Within America, there are a variety of records that can be used to find out information about the original immigrant ancestor. These include Immigration Records in the form of passenger lists and indexes. The lists normally include the name, age, sex, occupation and origin of the passenger, even if he or she died in passage. Unfortunately, these lists are by no means comprehensive. They are held in the National Archives, Washington, although the National Archives in Dublin and the Public Record Office in Northern Ireland have microfilm copies of a number of them.

Naturalisation Papers

These are generally held locally in the District Courts. They frequently include detailed information on age, nationality (sometimes given as precise place of origin) and whether citizenship was granted.

Census Returns

A population census of the United States has been taken every ten years since 1790. They vary, however, in the information they contain. These records are available in the National Archives in Washington. Unfortunately, part of the 1890 census was destroyed by fire in 1921.

Mortality Schedules

These are lists of deaths in a locality in a given year, based on information found in the census returns. They usually include the place of birth and are housed in the National Archives, Washington.

Military Service Records

The National Archives holds registers of US Army enlistments between 1798 and 1914. They include a full dossier on each recruit.

Land Records

This miscellaneous collection of records covers the period 1800-1950 and includes homestead applications and land claims as well as the relevant documents supporting these claims. These records are held in the National Archives.

Passport Records

These occasionally provide the precise place of origin of an ancestor. They are available from the Research and Liaison Branch, Passport Department, Department of State, Washington DC.

Births, Deaths and Marriages

Some states began registration early in the 19th century, but generally it did not commence until 1890. The one exception to this is marriage records, which often date back to the 18th century. For information prior to registration, it is necessary to consult church records, usually held in local custody.

Useful Addresses

The U.S. National Archives and Records Administration
8601 Adelphi Road, College Park, MD 20740-6001
Telephone: +1 86 NARA NARA or +1 86 6272 6272
Website: www.archives.gov

The U.S. Department of State
2201 C St NW, Washington DC 20520, USA
Telephone: +1 20 2647 4000
Website: www.state.gov

Canada

Large-scale emigration from Europe to Canada did not begin until the middle of the 18th century. This was due largely to frequent attacks on any new settler groups by the native Indians. However, the establishment of a chain of French military outposts helped to bring to an end this period of instability, and encouraged large numbers of people from Ireland, Britain and France to emigrate to Canada.

Emigration from Ireland to Canada reached its peak in the first half of the 19th century when over 500,000 Irish people chose to settle there. By 1901 approximately one million Canadians claimed Irish ancestry. The main attraction of Canada for immigrants was that land was cheap and in plentiful supply.

As early as the 18th century there were instances of organised emigration from Ireland. For example, Alexander Nutt, a native of Donegal, brought a group of Irish Protestants to settle in Nova Scotia in a place that became known as the Londonderry Settlement. The success of this venture encouraged other groups to follow: by 1766 there were approximately 1,000 Irish people in the Londonderry area. Irish emigrants were soon to be found in all parts of Canada.

Emigrants to Canada came from a wide variety of backgrounds. An undoubted advantage of choosing this location was the relative cheapness of the journey. Canada was the closest British colony to Ireland, which made the cost of passage less expensive than that of other destinations. Many of the early passengers were simply regarded as ballast on empty timber ships returning to Canada. It is not surprising that conditions of passage were not very good. There was, inevitably, disease and sickness amongst the passengers and, in 1832, the infamous Grosse Island in Quebec was established as a quarantine station for immigrants. After the 1850s, emigration to Canada became less popular as an increasing number of emigrants chose the United States of America as their destination. Although, due to the cheapness of the Canadian fare, many emigrants sailed first to Canada and then made their way overland to the United States. These migrants can be harder to identify.

Records for family research in Canada are similar to those available in Ireland, the main categories being records of civil registrations of births, deaths and marriages and census returns. Unlike Irish records, however, these records were not centralised but collected at the provincial level so they vary considerably in the amount of information they contain and the date they begin. Census returns for the provinces of Nova Scotia and Newfoundland, for example, date back to the 17th century, whereas those for British Columbia and Alberta did not start until the late 19th century.

Passenger lists are very rare, although a very useful book has been compiled by Brian Mitchell entitled *Irish Passenger Lists, 1847-71*, that details passengers sailing from Londonderry to North America on the ships of the J. & J. Cooke and the McCorkell lines.

Useful Addresses
Library and Archives Canada
395 Wellington St Ottawa, ON K1A 0N4
Telephone: +1 613 996 7458
Website: www.collectionscanada.gc.ca

Nova Scotia Archives & Records Management
6016 University Avenue, Halifax, Nova Scotia, B3H 1W4
Telephone: +1 90 2424 6060
Website: www.gov.ns.ca/nsarm

Public Archives and Records Office of Prince Edward Island
Hon. George Coles Building, 4th floor, 175 Richmond St,
Charlottetown PE, C1A 1H8
Telephone: +1 90 2368 4290
Website: http://www.gov.pe.ca/cca/index.
    php3?number=1004626

Archives nationales du Québec
85 Rue Sainte-Therese, Montreal, Quebec, H2Y 1E4
Telephone: +1 418 727 3500
Website: www.banq.qc.ca/portal/dt/genealogie/

Provincial Archives of Alberta
8555 Roper Road, Edmonton, AB T6E 5W1
Telephone: +1 780 427 1750
Website: www.culture.alberta.ca/archives

Provincial Archives of British Columbia
655 Belleville St, Victoria, British Columbia, V8W 9W2
Telephone: +1 250 387 1952
Website: www.bcarchives.bc.ca

Australia

The Australian bicentennial celebrations in 1988 increased
awareness of the long-established links between Australia

and Ireland. In 1788, the transportation of convicts from Britain to Australia (or New South Wales as it was then known) began, and the first ship full of Irish convicts sailed from Cork in 1791. Despite the early reputation of Australia being a land of 'convicts and kangaroos', by 1820 the country contained a broad mixture of immigrants, only about one eighth of the residents having a criminal past. During the Great Famine of 1845-52, emigration to Australia increased. During this time, the governments of Britain and Australia collaborated on a scheme to send young orphaned girls, whose families had died as a result of the Famine, to Australia. The scheme was short-lived and beset with scandal. As a consequence, about 4,000 Irish females migrated to Australia in the latter years of the Famine. The Irish immigrants to Australia made a significant contribution to the continent's development, from the bush-ranging Ned Kelly and Jack Donoghue to the more respectable John O'Shanassy, Sir Patrick Jennings and Paul Keating, each of whom became premiers.

Records in Australia

As a result of the federalist structure of Australia, official statistics started at different stages in each state. The state registration of births, deaths and marriages, for example, started in Tasmania in 1838, while state registration of these records did not begin in New South Wales until 1856. These certificates contain excellent information for the family historian. The New South Wales death certificate is particularly useful as it gives the following details:

> name, age, address and occupation of the deceased
> date and place of death and burial
> name and occupation of the father of the deceased
> maiden name of the deceased's mother
> the deceased's birthplace and the number of years he
>   or she had lived in the state
> the name of his or her spouse
> the date and place of marriage

age at time of marriage
names of the deceased's children, their ages and
   whether they were still living.

These certificates contain much more information than their equivalent in Ireland and are an excellent resource for tracing ancestors who migrated to Australia.

Unfortunately, many 19th-century census returns were destroyed by government order shortly after they were collected. Exceptions to this are the New South Wales Census for 1828 and the Tasmania Census for 1852.

Church records generally begin in the early part of the 19th century and are usually kept by the Registrar General of each state. Shipping records are also held by the appropriate state archives. Although they vary in the information they contain, usually they provide:

name
age
marital status
occupation
birthplace in Ireland.

State Records New South Wales has the most comprehensive collection of records relating to emigrants, whether they came as convicts or government-assisted settlers. This Record Office has provided excellent guides to its collections including *Guide to the Convict Records in the Archives Office, New South Wales* and *Guide to Shipping and Free Passenger Records*. Unfortunately, as is so often the case, few records survive for the majority of early emigrants. Within Ireland, records relating to settlement in Australia are relatively scarce. Transportation registers began in 1836 and for the period before this, the only way to trace an errant ancestor may be in a local newspaper report. It is generally considered easier, therefore, to work with the Australian records.

A useful although not comprehensive book has been produced by H.W. Coffey and M. Morgan entitled *Irish Families in Australia and New Zealand, 1788-1985*. This publication includes brief histories of approximately 10,000 Irish settlers from a range of social backgrounds. It is available in most reference libraries.

Useful Addresses
State Records New South Wales
PO Box 516, Kingswood, NSW 2747, New South Wales
Telephone: +61 2 9673 1788
Website: www.records.nsw.gov.au/staterecords

National Archives of Australia
PO Box 7425, Canberra,
ACT 2610, Australian Crown Territories
Telephone: + 61 2 6212 3900
Website: www.naa.gov.au

State Library, Archives Branch
State Library of Western Australia
Alexander Library Building, Perth Cultural Centre
Perth, WA 6000, Western Australia
Telephone: +61 8 9427 3111
Website: www.slwa.wa.gov.au/famhist.html

State Library, Archives Department
The State Library of South Australia, GPO Box 419, Adelaide,
SA 5001, South Australia
Telephone: +61 8 8207 7250
Website: www.slsa.sa.gov.au

Archives Office
Queensland State Archives, 435 Compton Road, Runcorn,
Brisbane, QLD 4113, Queensland
Telephone: +61 7 3131 7777
Website: www.archives.qld.gov.au

State Library of Tasmania, Archives Department
91 Murray St, Hobart, TAS 7000, Tasmania
Telephone: +61 3 6233 7511
Website: www.statelibrary.tas.gov.au

State Library of Victoria, Archives Division
304-324, Swanston St, Melbourne, VIC 3000, Victoria
Telephone: +61 3 8664 7000
Website: www.slv.vic.gov.au

State Archives of New South Wales
Macquarie St, Sydney, NSW 2000, New South Wales
Telephone: +61 2 9273 1414
Website: www.records.nsw.gov.au/archives

Public and Church Records
The Registrar-General
State Library of Western Australia, Alexander Library Building,
Perth Cultural Centre, Perth, WA 6000, Western Australia
Telephone: +61 8 9427 3111
Website: www.slwa.wa.gov.au

The Principal Registrar
1 Gouger St, Adelaide, SA 5000, South Australia
Telephone: +61 8 8204 0476
Website: www.courts.sa.gov.au

The Registrar-General
110 George St, Brisbane, QLD 4000, Queensland
Telephone: +61 3 0036 6430
Website: www.justice.qld.gov.au/16.htm

The Registrar-General
91 Murray St, Hobart, TAS 7001, Tasmania
Telephone: +61 3 6233 7488
Website: www.search.archives.tas.gov.au

The Registrar-General
Department of Justice, 121 Exhibition St, GPO Box 4356,
Melbourne, VIC 3000, Victoria
Telephone: +61 3 8684 0000
Website: www.justice.vic.gov.au

The Registrar-General
Prince Albert Road, Sydney, NSW 2000, New South Wales
Telephone: +61 2 9354 1370
Website: www.bdm.nsw.gov.au

The Registrar-General
Parkes Place, Parkes, ACT 2600, Australian Crown
Territories
or
PO Box 6309, Kingston, ACT 2604, Australian Crown
Territories
Telephone: +61 2 6270 6857
Website: www.hcourt.gov.au/registry_01.html

New Zealand

Although the links between New Zealand and Ireland have
received relatively little attention, there has been a long
history of emigration to that country. In February 1840, the
Treaty of Waitangi was introduced, paving the way for white
emigrants to settle in 'Maori land'. This date marks the
beginning of the organised colonisation of New Zealand by
British settlers. Irish people were an important part of this
group and, by 1890, those born in Ireland made up almost
twenty per cent of the non-Maori population. Many of these
immigrants were funded by the Australian government during
the so-called Vogel Era of the 1880s and 1890s. A scarcity of
women led to them being in great demand, not least for their
domestic abilities, and schemes were set up to encourage
them to settle in New Zealand.

The links between Ireland and New Zealand were further
strengthened when, in 1891, John Ballance, who was born
in Glenavy, County Antrim, became Prime Minister. Ballance,

affectionately known as 'The Rainmaker', was remarkable in many ways: under his premiership women were given the vote, New Zealand being the first country to grant this right. The publication; *Irish Families in Australia and New Zealand, 1788-1985* by H.W. Coffey and M. Morgan, can be a useful source of information relating to ancestors who may have emigrated to New Zealand.

Useful Addresses

Archives New Zealand
PO Box 12-050, Wollington
or
10 Mulgrave St, Thorndon, Wellington 6011, New Zealand
Telephone: +64 4499 5595
Website: www.archives.govt.nz

The Registrar-General
Registry of Births, Deaths and Marriages
PO Box 10-526, Wellington 6143
or
Level 3, Boulcott House, 47 Boulcott St, Wellington 6011, New Zealand
Telephone: +64 4474 8150
Website: www.bdm.govt.nz

New Zealand Society of Genealogists
PO Box 14036, Panmure, Auckland 1741, New Zealand
Telephone: +64 9570 4248
Website: www.genealogy.org.nz

Australasian Federation of Family History Organisations Inc.
PO Box 3012, Weston Creek
ACT 2611, Australian Crown Territories
Telephone: +64 0400 91 3866 [mobile number]
Website: www.affho.org/affho/members.php

New Zealand Family History Library
PO Box 1467, Wellington 6140
or
Cnr Molesworth and Aitken Streets, Wellington, New Zealand
Telephone: +64 4474 3000
Website: www.natlib.govt.nz

Getting Started: The Essential Steps

1. Start in your own home. Make a list of the information that you already know. Find further details from members of your family and by searching through family memorabilia. All of this information should be verified at a later date by checking it against official sources.

2. Visit your local reference library. Find out as much as possible about the surnames and the places being investigated. See what other records the library has – published pedigrees and family histories can be particularly useful.

3. Begin a search in the official records, such as the Registry of Births, Deaths and Marriages. Search these records as far back as possible, obtaining copies of certificates whenever you can. The information that you find here will make a search of other records possible – for example, wills, newspapers, obituaries, census returns and parish registers.

4. When you have established where your ancestors lived at the turn of the century, search the 1901 and 1911 census returns.

5. From birth, death and marriage certificates you should know your ancestor's address in the 1860s. Griffith's *Valuation* will provide information about the type of property they lived in. The Tithe Applotment Books will provide information about the family in the 1820s.

6. By now you should have established the religion and the address of your ancestor for the period before 1864. Search the relevant parish records as far back as possible for information on baptisms, marriages and burials.

7. The information in the parish registers can be supplemented with details from other sources such as wills, gravestone inscriptions, school registers, etc.

8. For the 18th century and earlier, sources become more scattered and less comprehensive. Check as wide a range of records as you can, including newspapers, estate records, the Registry of Deeds, etc.

While the above steps are the most obvious to take, you must remember that each family history is individual and does not conform to any one pattern. Some of the records mentioned may not yield the requisite information, in which case the less obvious sources may prove to be more useful. The more extensive the range of sources you use, the higher will be your ultimate chance of success. Throughout the course of your search, remember:

Write everything down.
Start with your own family and then work back
systematically, generation by generation.
Bear in mind the possible variants of the spelling in
names and surnames.
If you come to an apparent standstill, do not
give up. Approach the search in different ways,
perhaps by concentrating on another branch of
the family.

Useful Addresses

In The Republic Of Ireland

Dublin Public Library and Archives Department
138-144 Pearse St, Dublin 2
Telephone: +353 (0) 1 674 4800
Website: www.dublincity.ie

The Genealogical Office
The National Library
Kildare St, Dublin 2
Telephone: +353 (0) 1 603 0200
Website: www.nli.ie

The General Valuation Office
Irish Life Centre, Abbey St Lower, Dublin 1
Telephone: +353 (0) 1 817 1000
Website: www.valoff.ie

The National Archives
(formerly, the Public Record Office of Ireland)
8 Bishop St, Dublin 8
Telephone: +353 (0) 1 407 2300
Fax: +353 (0) 1 407 2333
Website: www.nationalarchives.ie

The National Library
Kildare St, Dublin 2
Telephone: + 353 (0) 1 603 0200
Website: www.nli.ie

Place Names Commission
Dún Aimhirgin, 43-49 Mespil Road, Dublin 4
Telephone: +353 (0) 1 647 3000
Website: www.pobail.ie

Ordnance Survey Office
Phoenix Park, Dublin 8
Telephone: +353 (0) 1 820 6100
Website: www.osi.ie

The Property Registration Authority
(formerly the Registry of Deeds)
Chancery St, Dublin 7
Telephone: +353 (0) 1 670 7500
Website: www.prai.ie

General Register Office
Government Offices, Convent Road, Roscommon
Telephone: +353 (0) 90 663 2900
Website: www.groireland.ie

Library of the Representative Church Body
The Representative Body of the Church of Ireland
Braemor Park, Churchtown, Dublin 14
Telephone: +353 (0) 1 492 3979
Website: www.ireland.anglican.org

Royal Irish Academy
19 Dawson St, Dublin 2
Telephone: +353 (0) 1 676 2570
Website: www.ria.ie

Society of Friends Meeting House
Historical Library, Stocking Lane, Rathfarnham, Dublin 16
Telephone: +353 (0) 1 495 6890
Website: www.quakers-in-ireland.ie

In Northern Ireland

Presbyterian Historical Society
Church House, Fisherwick Place, Belfast BT1 6DW
Telephone: +44 (0) 28 9032 2284
Website: www.presbyterianhistoryireland.com

Public Record Office of Northern Ireland
66 Balmoral Avenue, Belfast BT9 6NY
Telephone: +44 (0) 28 9025 1318
Website: www.proni.gov.uk

Registrar General of Northern Ireland
Oxford House, 49-55 Chichester St, Belfast BT1 4HL
Telephone: +44 (0) 28 9025 2000
Website: www.groni.gov.uk

Libraries and Family History Research Centres in Northern Ireland

Armagh Ancestry
42 English St, Armagh BT61 7BA
Telephone: +44 (0) 28 3752 1800
Website: www.armagh.brsgenealogy.com

The Association of Ulster Genealogists and Record Agents
Glen Cottage, Glenmachan Road, Belfast BT4 2NP
Email: secretary@augra.com
Website: www.augra.com

Belfast Public Libraries
Central Library, Royal Avenue, Belfast BT1 1EA
Telephone: +44 (0) 28 9050 9167
Website: www.ni-libraries.net

Derry Genealogy Centre
10-16 Pump St, Londonderry RT48 6JG
Telephone: +44 (0) 28 7126 0329
Website: www.irishgenealogy.ie

Irish Heritage Association
15-17 Portview, 310 Newtownards Road, Belfast BT4 1HE
Telephone: +44 (0) 28 9045 5325
Website: www.irishgenealogy.ie

The Ulster Historical Foundation
Unit 7, Cotton Court, Waring St, Belfast BT1 2ED
Telephone: +44 (0) 28 9033 2288
Website: www.ancestryireland.com

Education and Library Boards in Northern Ireland

Belfast Education and Library Board
Belfast Public Libraries, Central Library,
Royal Avenue, Belfast BT1 1EA
Telephone: +44 (0) 28 9050 9161
Website: www.ni-libraries.net

North Eastern Education and Library Board
Library Service and Area Library, 5 Pat's Brae, Ballymena,
Co. Antrim, BT43 5AX
Telephone: +44 (0) 28 2563 3950
Website: www.ni-libraries.net

South Eastern Education and Library Board
Library Headquarters, Windmill Hill, Ballynahinch,
Co. Down, BT24 8DH
Telephone: +44 (0) 28 9756 6400
Website: www.ni-libraries.net

Southern Education and Library Board
39c Abbey St, Armagh, Co. Armagh BT61 7EB
Telephone: +44 (0) 28 3752 7851
Website: www.ni-libraries.net

Western Education and Library Board
Library Headquarters, Spillars Place, Omagh,
Co. Tyrone BT78 1HL
Telephone: +44 (0) 28 8224 4821
Website: www.ni-libraries.net

Libraries and Family History Research Centres in the Republic of Ireland

The Association of Professional Genealogists in Ireland
Hon. Secretary, 30 Harlech Crescent, Clonskeagh, Dublin 14
Telephone: +353 (0) 1 496 6522
Email: info@apgi.ie
Website: www.apgi.ie

Bru Boru Heritage Centre
Cashel, Co. Tipperary
Telephone: +353 (0) 62 61122
Website: www.comhaltas.ie/locations/detail/bru_boru

Carlow County Library
Carlow Local Authorities, County Buildings, Athy Road,
Carlow Town, Co. Carlow
Telephone: +353 (0) 59 917 0300
Website: www.carlow.ie/Information/LibraryServices

Cavan County Library
Farnham St, Cavan, Co. Cavan
Telephone: +353 (0) 49 437 8500
Website: wwww.cavancoco.ie

County Cavan Genealogical Research Centre
1st Floor, Johnston Central Library, Farnham St,
Cavan, Co. Cavan
Telephone: 353 (0) 49 436 1094
Website: www.irish-roots.ie/cavan.asp

Clare County Library
County Library Headquarters, Mill Road, Ennis, Co. Clare
Telephone: +353 (0) 65 684 6350
Website: www.clarelibrary.ie

Clare Heritage Centre
Church St, Corofin, Co. Clare
Telephone: +353 (0) 65 683 7955
Website: www.clareroots.com

Cork City Library
57-61 Grand Parade, Cork City, Co. Cork
Telephone: +353 (0) 21 492 4900
Website: www.corkcitylibraries.ie

Cork County Library
Library Headquarters, Model Business Park,
Model Farm Road, Cork
Telephone: +353 (0) 21 454 6499
Website: www.corkcoco.ie

Donegal County Library
Central Library, High Road, Letterkenny, Co. Donegal
Telephone: +353 (0) 74 912 1968
Website: www.donegal.ie/library

Donegal Ancestry Centre
The Quay, Ramelton, Letterkenny, Co. Donegal
Telephone: +353 (0) 74 915 1266
Website: www.donegalancestry.com

Dublin County Libraries
South Dublin County Council, County Hall,
Tallaght, Dublin 24
Telephone: +353 (0) 1 414 9000
Website: www.southdublinlibraries.ie

Dublin Heritage Service
Education and Visitor Service, 51 St. Stephens Green,
Dublin 2
Telephone: +353 (0) 1 661 3111
Website: www.opw.ie

Dun Laoghaire/Rathdown Heritage Project
County Hall, Marine Road, Dún Laoghaire, Co. Dublin
Telephone: +353 (0) 1 205 4700
www.dlrcoco.ie/heritage

Dun na Si Heritage Centre
Knockdowney, Moate, Co. Westmeath
Telephone: +353 (0) 90 648 1183
Website: www.irishtourist.com/details/dun_na_si_heritage_
    centre_and_park.shtml

Galway County Libraries
County Library Headquarters, Island House,
Cathedral Square, Galway, Co. Galway
Telephone: +353 (0) 91 50 9000
Website: www.galway.ie/en/services/library

Galway East Family History Society Ltd
Woodford Heritage Centre, Woodford, Co. Galway
Telephone: + 353 (0) 90 974 9309
Website: www.irish-roots.ie/galway-east.asp

Galway West Family History Society
St. Joseph's Community Centre, Shantalla, Co. Galway
Telephone: +353 (0) 91 86 0464
Website: www.irish-roots.ie/galway-west.asp

Irish Family History Society
PO Box 36, Naas, Co. Kildare
Telephone: +353 (0) 1 831 0848
Website: http://homepage.eircom.net/~ifhs/

Kerry County Library
Tralee, Co. Kerry
Telephone: +353 (0) 66 712 1200
Website: http://www.kerrycolib.ie/

Kildare Heritage Project
Riverbank Arts Centre, Main St, Newbridge, Co. Kildare
Telephone: +353 (0) 45 43 1109
Website: www.kildare.ie/library

Kilkenny County Library
Library Headquarters and Local Studies
6 Rose Inn St, Kilkenny, Co. Kilkenny
Telephone: +353 (0) 56 779 4160
Website: http://kilkennylibrary.kilkenny.ie

Laois County Library
Library Headquarters,
County Hall, James Fintan Lalor Avenue,
Portlaoise, Co. Laois
Telephone: +353 (0) 57 867 4315
Website: www.laois.ie/LeisureandCulture/Libraries

Laois and Offaly Family History Research
Bury Quay, Tullamore, Co. Offaly
Telephone: + 353 (0) 057 932 1421
Website: www.irishmidlandsancestry.com

Leitrim County Library
Ballinamore, Co. Leitrim
Telephone: +353 (0) 71 964 5582
Website: www.leitrimcoco.ie/Departments/Library

Leitrim Genealogy Centre
c/o County Library, Ballinamore, Co. Leitrim
Telephone: +353 (0) 71 964 5582
Website: www.leitrimcoco.ie/Departments/Library

Limerick County Library
58 O'Connell St, Limerick, Co. Limerick
Telephone: +353 (0) 61 21 4452
Website: www.lcc.ie/Library

Limerick Regional Archives
Limerick County Council, County Hall, Dooradoyle,
Co. Limerick
Telephone: +353 (0) 61 49 6000
Website: www.lcc.ie/Library

Longford County Library
Arts, Archives and Heritage Services, Longford,
Co. Longford
Telephone: +353 (0) 43 41124
Website: www.longfordlibrary.ie

Longford Roots
Longford Roots Research Centre, 17 Dublin St, Longford,
Co. Longford
Telephone: +353 (0) 43 41235
Website: www.longford.ie

Louth County Library
Archives, Old Gaol, Ardee Road, Dundalk, Co. Louth
Telephone: +353 (0) 42 933 9387
Website: www.louthcoco.ie

Mallow Heritage Centre
27-8 Bank Place, Mallow, Co. Cork
Telephone: +353 (0) 22 50302
Website: www.mallowheritagecentre.com

Mayo County Library
Library Headquarters,
John Moore Road, Castlebar, Co. Mayo
Telephone: +353 (0) 94 904 7922
Website: www.mayolibrary.ie

Mayo North Family History Research Centre
Enniscoe, Castlehill, Ballina, Co. Mayo
Telephone: +353 (0) 96 31809
Website: www.mayo.irishroots.net

Mayo South Family Research Centre
Main St, Ballinrobe, Co. Mayo
Telephone: +353 (0) 94 954 1214
Website: www.mayo.irishroots.net

Meath County Library
Railway St, Navan, Co. Meath
Telephone: +353 (0) 46 909 7000
Website: www.meath.ie/LocalAuthorities/Libraries

Meath Heritage Centre
Town Hall, Castle St, Trim, Co. Meath
Telephone: +353 (0) 46 943 6633
Website: www.meathroots.com

Clones Branch Library
& Monaghan County Library Headquarters
The Diamond, Clones, Co. Monaghan
Telephone: +353 (0) 47 51143
Website: www.monaghan.ie/websitev2/libraries/
    history&genealogy.html

Offaly County Library
O'Connor Square, Tullamore, Co. Offaly
Telephone: +353 (0) 57 934 6834
Website: www.offaly.ie/offalyhome/culture/library

Roscommon County Library
Abbey St, Roscommon, Co. Roscommon
Telephone: +353 (0) 90 663 7274
Website: www.roscommoncoco.ie/services/library.html

Roscommon Heritage and Genealogical Centre
Church St, Strokestown, Co. Roscommon
Telephone: +353 (0) 71 963 3380
Website: www.roscommonroots.com

Sligo County Library
Headquarters, The Westward Town Centre, Bridge St,
Sligo, Co. Sligo
Telephone: +353 (0) 71 914 7190
Website: www.library.itsligo.ie

Sligo Heritage and Genealogical Centre
Aras Reddan, Temple St, Sligo, Co. Sligo
Telephone: +353 (0) 71 914 3728
Website: www.sligoroots.com

Tipperary Joint Library Committee
Castle Avenue, Thurles, Co. Tipperary
Telephone: +353 (0) 504 21555
Website: www.tipperarylibraries.ie

Tipperary North Family History Foundation
The Governor's House, Kickham St, Nenagh, Co. Tipperary
Telephone: +353 (0) 67 33850
Website: www.tipperarynorth.brsgenealogy.com

Waterford County Council Library Service
County Library Headquarters, Ballyanchor Road,
Lismore, Co. Waterford
Telephone: +353 (0) 58 21370
Website: www.waterfordcountylibrary.ie

Waterford Heritage Survey
Jenkins Lane, Waterford City, Co. Waterford
Telephone: +353 (0) 51 76123
Website: www.iol.ie/~mnoc

Local Studies Department (Archives)
Westmeath County Library Headquarters,
Dublin Road, Mullingar, Co. Westmeath
Telephone: +353 (0) 44 934 0781
Email: library@westmeathcoco.ie
Website: www.westmeathcoco.ie/servicesa-z/library/
    westmeathinthepast/archives/

Wexford County Archive Service
c/o Wexford Library Management Services,
6A Ardcavan Business Park, Ardcavan, Co. Wexford
Telephone: +353 (0) 53 912 4922
Website: www.wexford.ie/wex/Departments/Library

Wexford Heritage Research Centre
Yola Farmstead, Tagoat, Rosslare, Co. Wexford
Telephone: +353 (0) 53 913 2610
Website: www.homepage.eircom.net/~yolawexford/
    genealogy.htm

Wicklow County Library
Boghall Road, Bray, Co. Wicklow
Telephone: +353 (0) 1 286 6566
Website: www.wicklow.ie

Tracing Your Irish Roots

Wicklow Family History Centre
Wicklow's Historic Gaol
Killmantin Hill, Wicklow Town, Co. Wicklow
Telephone: +353 (0) 404 20126
Website: www.wicklow.ie/familyhistorycentre

Select Bibliography

Adolph, Anthony, *Tracing Your Irish Family History*, 2007

Bardon, Jonathan, *Guide to Local History Sources in the Public Record Office of Northern Ireland,* 2000

Barrington, Claire, *Irish women in England: an annotated bibliography*, 1997

Begley, D., *Irish Genealogy: A Record Finder*, 1981

Begley, D., *The Ancestral Trail in Ireland*, 1982

Bell, R., *The Book of Ulster Surnames*, 1997

Bonsall, Penny, *The Irish RMs: The Resident Magistrates in the British Administration of Ireland*, 1997

Burke, B., *Landed Gentry of Ireland*, 1980

Burke, Sir John Bernard, *A Genealogical and Heraldic History of the Landed Gentry of Ireland*, 1912

Clarke, R.S.J. (ed.) *Gravestone Inscriptions*, 1966 onwards (over 20 volumes have been published in this series covering counties Antrim and Down)

Coffey, H.W. and Morgan, M., *Irish Families in Australia and New Zealand 1788-1985*, 1986

Collins, Peter, *County Monaghan Sources in PRONI*, 1998

Crawford, E. Margaret (ed.), *The Hungry Stream: Essays on Emigration and Famine*, 1997

Dickson-Falley, M., *Irish and Scotch-Irish Ancestral Research*, 1995

Dublin Public Libraries, *A Directory of Graveyards in the Dublin Area: An Index and Guide to Burial Records*, 1990

Eustace, P.B., *Registry of Deeds, Dublin: Abstracts of Will Vol. 1, 1708-1745*

Eustace, P.B., *Registry of Deeds, Dublin: Abstracts of Will Vol. 2, 1746-1785*

Gallagher, C., Kinealy, C. and Parkhill, T., *Making Sense of History: Evidence in Ireland for the Young Historian*, 1995

Goodbody, O.C., *Guide to Irish Quaker Records* (revised ed.), 1999

Grehan, I., *Irish Family Names*, 2006

Grenham, John, *Tracing Your Irish Ancestors*, 2006

Griffin, Brian, *The Bulkies: Police and Crime in Belfast 1800-1865*, 1999

Hayes, R., *Manuscript Sources for the History of Irish Civilisation*, 1979

Heraldic Artists, *Handbook on Irish Genealogy*, 1984

Hyman, L., *The Jews in Ireland*, 1997

Killen, W.D., *History of Congregations of the Presbyterian Church in Ireland and Bibliographical Notices of Eminent Presbyterian Ministers and Laymen*, 1886

Kinealy, Christine, *A Disunited Kingdom? England, Ireland, Scotland and Wales, 1800-1949*, 1999

Kinealy, Christine, *This Great Calamity: The Irish Famine 1845-52*, 1994

Lewis, S.A., *Topographical Dictionary of Ireland*, 1837

MacLysaght, E., *Guide to Irish Surnames*, 1964

MacLysaght, E., *Irish Families: Their Names, Arms and Origins*, 1985

MacLysaght, E., *More Irish Families*, 1996

MacLysaght, E., *The Surnames of Ireland*, 1999

Matheson, R., *Varieties and Synonyms of Surnames and Christian Names in Ireland,* 1995

Maxwell, Ian, *How to Trace Your Irish Ancestors: An Essential Guide to Researching and Documenting the Family Histories of Ireland's People,* 2008

Maxwell, Ian, *Your Irish Ancestors: A Guide for the Family Historian,* 2008

McClaughlin, Trevor, *From Shamrock to Wattle*, 1985

Mitchell, Brian, *Finding Your Irish Ancestors: Unique Aspects of Irish Genealogy,* 2001

Mitchell, Brian, *Irish Passenger Lists, 1847-71*, 1988

Mitchell, Brian, *Pocket Guide to Irish Genealogy*, 2002

Morgan, M., *Irish Families in Australia and New Zealand 1788-1985*, 1986

Murphy, Hilary, *Families of County Wexford*, 1998

Presbyterian Historical Society, *A History of Congregations in the Presbyterian Church in Ireland 1610-1982*, 1982

Roulston, William, *Researching Scots-Irish Ancestors: The Essential Genealogical Guide to Early Modern Ulster*, 2005

Ryan, James G., *Irish Church Records*, 1992

Ryan, James G., *Irish Records: Sources for Family and Local History*, 1997

Ryan, James G., *Tracing your Dublin Ancestors*, 1988

Sexton, Sean, *Ireland. Photographs 1840-1930*, 1994

Shillman, B., *A Short History of the Jews in Ireland*, 1945

Swift, R. and Gilley, S., *The Irish in Britain, 1815-1939*, 1989

Trainor, Brian, *Research Irish Australians: Directory of Research with Will Abstracts and Gravestone Inscriptions*, 1998

Ulster Genealogy and Historical Guild, *Familia: Ulster Genealogical Review* (published annually)

Vicars, A., *Index to Prerogative Wills of Ireland 1536-1810*, 1837